BLACK AND WHITE AIRMEN

Their True History

AT ITALY 1944

www.houghtonmifflinbooks.com

The text of this book is set in Adobe Garamond Pro.
Photo credits appear on page 155.

Library of Congress Cataloging-in-Publication Data
Fleischman, John, 1948–
Black and white airmen: their true history / by John
Fleischman
p. cm.
Includes bibliographical references and index.
ISBN-13: 978-0-618-56297-8
ISBN-10: 0-618-56297-4
1. Leahr, John, 1920—Juvenile literature. 2.
Heilbrun, Herb, 1920—Juvenile literature. 3. United
States. Army Air Forces. Fighter Group, 332nd—
Biography—Juvenile literature. 4. United States.
Army Air Forces. Bombardment Group (Heavy),
301st—Biography—Juvenile literature. 5. World War,
1939–1945—Participation, African American—Juvenile
literature. 6. Air pilots, Military—United States—
Biography—Juvenile literature 7. African American
air pilots—Biography—Juvenile literature. 8. African
Americans—Social conditions—To 1964—Juvenile
literature 9. African American—Ohio—Cincinnati—
Social conditions—To 1964—Juvenile literature. I. Title
D790.252332nd .F64 2007
940.54'4973092396073—dc22 [B]   2006017059

Printed in Singapore
TWP 10 9 8 7 6 5 4 3

U.S. ARMY AIR FORCE

IDENTIFICATION CARD
УДОСТОВЕРЕНИЕ ЛИЧНОСТИ
DOWÓD OSOBISTY
LEGITIMACE

BLACK AND WHITE
AIRMEN

Their True History

JOHN FLEISCHMAN

HOUGHTON MIFFLIN COMPANY
BOSTON

FOR GIULIO WILLIAM,

FOR GRANDCHILDREN,

AND FOR PEACE EVERYWHERE

★ ★ ★

Contents

★ ★ ★

Mission Briefing

John Leahr was already eighty when I first met him in 2000, but he still drove like a World War II fighter pilot, meaning that he drove carefully but we got there quickly. We didn't have far to go, five miles through the suburban streets around Cincinnati, Ohio, to pick up Herb Heilbrun. Herb had also been a U.S. Army pilot in World War II. The two of them were going to give a speech at a local junior college about their war experiences, and I wanted to go along to see them in action. John offered to drive us to Herb's. Good pilots are creatures of habit. I'd noticed on the way over that John, though he was probably unaware of it, constantly scanned his dashboard gauges, his mirrors, and the road, alert for anything unexpected closing in on his cream-colored Cadillac.

When John glided the car safely to the curb, Herb was waiting outside his house but at the other end of his driveway. Herb was looking at something in his backyard where his lawn dropped away sharply into a wooded ravine. Halfway down the slope, a sweaty teenager was

Best of friends: Herb Heilbrun and John Leahr in 2004, sixty years after they flew together on World War II bombing missions and seventy-six years after they were classmates in Miss Pitchell's third grade.

his life with special platform shoes from the Veterans Administration that evened up his uneven legs. Uncle Jim said he didn't remember a thing about the Battle of the Bulge. Or that was what he said, anyway.

But all this talk about different generations can be deceptive. In families, generations don't always separate so neatly. My best friend in Cincinnati, Chot (his real name is Charles but don't call him that), is also a baby boomer. Yet Chot had an older sister, Carol, who was married to an older man who'd been a B-17 bomber pilot. Chot said that his brother-in-law, Herb Heilbrun, had the most amazing stories about flying bombing missions in Italy during the war. In families, history can be a lot closer than it appears.

That's how I heard about Herb and John and how I came to write this true history of a friendship that almost wasn't. I call it a "history" with a small "h." History with a capital "H" is mixed up in it—World War II, military aviation, and racism for starters—but this begins and ends as a history of two friends. John Leahr and Herb Heilbrun were born within seven months and a mile of each other in Cincinnati, Ohio, in 1920. Herb and John grew up in the same neighborhood, went to the same elementary school, and were in Miss Pitchell's third grade together in 1928. In the third grade, they were classmates, not friends, because Herb was white and John was black. In 1928, that was a gap too wide for Cincinnati schoolboys to cross. When John's family moved, the boys soon forgot about each other. This is where their story could have ended, but History with a capital "H" intervened. It took them nearly seventy years, a world war, and a civil rights revolution, but John and Herb did become best friends, at last.

This, then, is the true story of their friendship, but as I am the one writing this book, I need to declare what I mean by a "true" story. We have all sorts of "true" stories today that aren't entirely true. We have "reality" TV shows that don't have much to do with reality. We have movies that are "based on," "adapted from," or (my favorite) "inspired by" true stories. True books like this one are usually called "nonfiction," which is a funny word. All it guarantees is that this book is "not fiction," that is, that I didn't make it up entirely. Imagine if food were labeled that way; imagine that the ingredients listed on an ice cream wrapper said only "Not stones." This is my ingredients list: I started with John and Herb, who not only had great memories but great stacks of army records, family letters, and snapshots. They also had great patience with my questions. Beyond their personal stories and papers, I explored the paper mountain range of books and documents devoted to World War II. In this paper mountain range, entire peaks are devoted to World War II aviation, with narrow valleys devoted to the Tuskegee Airmen and to the other African Americans who served in the war. The Internet has even more. It is very easy to learn too much about World War II.

Fortunately, this is the true story not of World War II but of a friendship that began in 1928 and took a while to get going. The English writer L. P. Hartley once said, "The past is a foreign country; they do things differently there." In that long-ago foreign country where John and Herb grew up, what boys and girls wore, read, played with, dreamed about, and studied in school were different.

A big problem in writing true nonfiction is what to do about the dialogue, that is, the parts of the story that appear inside quotation marks. Quotations are supposed to report, word for word, what someone wrote or actually said. Quoting from letters or documents is easy. Quoting people as they talk, even if you have a tape recorder, can drive you crazy. As a journalist, I've transcribed many tape-recorded interviews. Believe me, what most people really say, word for word, isn't pretty. People don't finish sentences. They don't finish thoughts. They don't finish stories. They tell you stories backwards or in pieces. Sometimes they tell you things in all sincerity that aren't true or that didn't happen in the way they remember. Writers—and readers—have to judge for themselves. Here are the rules for this book: all quotes are either from documents, from words I heard myself, or from John and Herb quoting someone else. There were no tape recorders running in Alabama in 1943 when John nearly washed out of army flight school. This is his version of what was said.

Now about the actual words in this story: some of them are ugly, particularly the racial and ethnic slurs. The words Americans use to describe race have changed since John and Herb were born and will likely keep changing. You can see them change in this story from "African" to "colored" to "Negro" to "black" to "African American." This is another way that the past is a foreign country; they speak other languages there.

The ugly ethnic slurs also belong to this story. They go with another ugly word, genocide, that comes out of World War II. It means a systematic killing program to exterminate an entire national or ethnic group. What we call the Holocaust today was the attempted genocide of the Jewish people of Europe by Adolf Hitler and his Nazi government. But Hitler targeted other ethnic groups for genocide, including the Romany people that we call the Gypsies. Genocide is targeted murder. Hitler's genocide killed millions, but indifference and bad luck killed millions more during the war. Mostly they were civilians who were left to die of hunger, disease, cold, or heat, or killed for being in the wrong place at the wrong time.

This story is also about the most violent and bloody conflict in human history. Even historians can't agree on just how many people were killed in World War II. One reliable estimate of the war dead is 55 million, including 30.5 million civilians. Counting the dead is only one historical controversy from the World War II, and this story touches on others. But the story of Herb and John makes sense only against this backdrop of terrible violence and ugly words. Fortunately, their story doesn't end there.

Everything in this book comes from a source, but there are no source notes sprinkled through the text. I leave source notes to scholars who write about History. I've listed my most useful story sources at the back of this book, plus some suggestions on where to look for more information. With all these ingredients, rules, and notes, there are probably mistakes in this "true" story. There are certainly unanswered questions. The mistakes are all mine. The true story is from John and Herb. The questions are for you.

CHAPTER ONE
Old Friends

Herb Heilbrun saved nearly everything. From his school days, Herb saved report cards and class photos. From his days in the real estate business, Herb saved files, listings, and every canceled check he ever wrote. From his days in the U.S. Army Air Forces during World War II, Herb saved the diary he kept as a B-17 bomber pilot and a piece of steel shrapnel the size of his thumb, one of eighty-nine fired by German antiaircraft guns that tore through his bomber on Christmas Day, 1944, during an attack on an oil refinery at Brux, Czechoslovakia. Herb saved his pilot's wings, air service ribbons, and canvas flying helmet, complete with goggles and rubber oxygen mask.

Herb even saved the manufacturer's manual that came with the brand-new four-engine, propeller-driven B-17 Model G "Flying Fortress" bomber that he picked up at Lincoln Army Airfield in Lincoln, Nebraska, on October 9, 1944. Herb's birthday was October 11, so when Second Lieutenant Herbert M. Heilbrun signed the delivery papers for B-17G airplane number 44-6631, he thought to himself that this was a fantastic twenty-fourth birthday present. The delivery price—$236,000—was an unimaginably large

Airmen: Lt. John H. Leahr (left) and Lt. Herbert M. Heilbrun (right), United States Army Air Forces.

sum of money in 1944, especially for Herb, who'd grown up in Cincinnati, Ohio, during the never-ending hard times of the Great Depression. Now here were 236,000 dollars wrapped up in one bright aluminum airplane.

Legally, both the B-17G and Lieutenant Heilbrun belonged to the flying branch of the U.S. Army Air Forces (or as it was known in the army's alphabet-speak, the AAF). But Herb wondered: What if he crashed this new B-17G? Would an angry Uncle Sam come after him for $236,000? Herb decided that if he survived the crash, he could pay off the bomber in installments: $2.36 a week times forever.

The B-17G was not a birthday present. Still, Herb was wild to take this shiny new machine for a ride after twenty-one long months of flying

An air cadet at last, Herb stands next to his Stearman "Kaydet" PT-17 in Primary training in early 1943. Herb had feared that he would be called up too late to fly in combat. As it happened, Herb arrived in plenty of time.

lessons. His army flying instructions had begun in a single-engine Primary trainer, a Stearman "Kaydet" PT-17 biplane. The Stearman had canvas-covered wings, a wooden propeller, and two open cockpits. Herb sat in the back cockpit and the instructor in the front until the day his instructor climbed out and told Herb to take the Stearman up solo. From a Primary trainer, Herb moved up to a Basic trainer, the Vultee BT-13, an all-metal single-engine monoplane with a glass canopy that enclosed both student and teacher. The Vultee was slow and steady, but so bumpy in tight turns that the cadets nicknamed it the "Vultee Vibrator."

In Basic training, Herb learned instrument flying in a special BT-13 fitted with a folding cloth blackout hood. The instructor, sitting in the back seat, could rig it over the student's head so that

Herb couldn't see anything but the flight gauges and dials in front of him. First Herb learned to fly the BT-13 eyes open. Then the instructor lowered the cloth hood so Herb could learn to fly blind, relying totally on instruments. This was preparation for bad weather and for night flying. In the rushing darkness, a military pilot couldn't see a thing beyond his wingtips. Only his instruments could tell him if his plane was flying level with the horizon at 10,000 feet or upside down 100 feet off the ground. From Basic, Herb graduated to Advanced "multiengine" training, starting on twin-engine AT-17 Cessna Bobcats, and finally to four-engine B-17 trainers. These were old, tired B-17s—obsolete early models, patched-up wrecks, or well-worn combat survivors—all painted the old Army Air Corps brown.

But Herb's new B-17G was no trainer. It was delivered direct from the Boeing factory in unpainted, polished aluminum. When the AAF and Boeing were planning the new Model G, engineers calculated that it took fifty pounds of paint to cover a B-17. Trimming away even fifty pounds of unnecessary weight would allow an unpainted B-17G to fly a little faster or a little higher. Against German antiaircraft guns, altitude and speed were better protection than paint. The AAF ordered all its new bombers in bare aluminum. When Herb climbed aboard his B-17G in Nebraska for the first

Herb was fresh from bomber training and in top physical shape in 1944. Herb liked to show off by hoisting crew members overhead.

time, it was so new that he noticed wet paint on the wooden floorboards. Airplanes don't have odometers, the instruments in automobiles that say how far a car has been driven. Airplanes measure their mileage by how many hours their engines have run. In 1944, a B-17 engine with five hundred hours "on the clock" was ready for a rebuild. When Herb checked his B-17G engines, they had six hours and fifteen minutes on the clock—the flying time from Seattle, Washington, where the plane was built, to Lincoln, Nebraska, where it was delivered. In automobile terms, his B-17G was fresh off the showroom floor and once round the block.

After inventorying equipment, calibrating instruments, and checking the guns, Herb and his crew took their B-17G up for a short "acceptance flight." Herb then reported his plane and crew ready for movement to an "Overseas Destination." Three days later, in the very, very early hours of the morning, an army clerk handed Herb his typed orders. They began, "You are assigned to Shipment No. FN-015-AY, as crew number FN-015-AY8 and to B-17 airplane number 44-6631, on aircraft project number 90946R." As commander and pilot, Lieutenant Heilbrun was to take the aforementioned aircraft and crew to "North Atlantic Wing, ATC, Grenier Field, Manchester, New Hampshire, or such other Air Port or Embarkation as the CG, ATC, may direct, thence to the overseas destination of Shipment FN-015-AY." In English, the orders meant they would fly alone to Grenier Field or to some "other Air Port of Embarkation," most likely in Canada, and await new orders. Herb knew that the next leg of the journey would be across the Atlantic Ocean to a B-17 squadron already flying combat missions somewhere in Europe. Exactly where he and his crew were going was a military secret. Movement orders were always secret. This was to confuse the enemy, although it usually confused the crewmen more.

It was six-thirty in the morning and still dark outside the operations building when Herb came out with the paperwork. His crew was waiting for him, their canvas duffel bags packed and stacked, ready to go. The sun wouldn't be up for another hour, yet Lincoln Field was already boiling with activity. Tanker trucks, taxiing aircraft, flight crews, jeeps, ground crews, crash vehicles, squads of marching airmen, and drab green Buick staff cars all swirled by. Nobody paid much attention to Herb and his crew. It took ten men to fly a B-17G in combat: four officers—pilot, copilot, bombardier, and navigator—and six enlisted men—radio operator, flight engineer, and four gunners. They were all young men. Lieutenant Heilbrun was the "old man" at twenty-four (and one day). The youngest were the gunners, teenagers fresh from high school into aerial gunnery school. Herb's men were from all backgrounds, all religions, and all over America. And they were all white, a situation that Herb and most white Americans in 1944 regarded as perfectly normal.

Herb trained on older B-17s like this Model F, still wearing its drab coat of AAF brown. But the basic crew layout was the same on the later B-17G. First in the nose was the bombardier (1), followed by the navigator's station (2). The pilot (3) had the left-hand seat on the flight deck, the copilot (4) the right. Directly behind them was the flight engineer (5), the senior noncommissioned officer on board who also served as top turret gunner. The radio operator's station (6) was behind the bomb bay, close to the hatch used by the bottom ball turret gunner (7). The two waist gunners, right (8) and left (9), fired through open hatches. They were the most exposed to high-altitude cold. The tail gunner (10) crawled through a tunnel to reach his position, tucked in under the B-17's massive tail rudder.

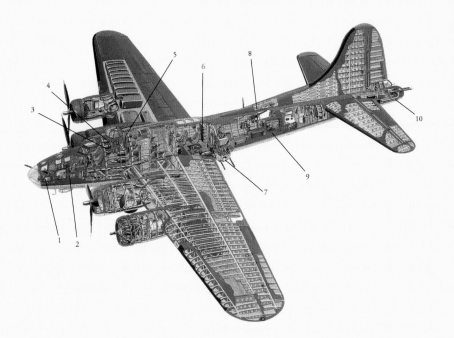

In 1944, the U.S. Armed Forces were strictly segregated. African Americans had fought as soldiers and sailors in every American war from the Revolution through the Spanish-American War in 1898. But the army's top generals were steeped in the official racism of the time that regarded Africans, Asians, Native Americans, and Hispanics as inferior human beings. By 1900, American generals had convinced themselves that African American soldiers would be "unfit" for the new twentieth-century warfare of rapid-fire guns, motor vehicles, field telephones, and high explosives.

In truth, the generals themselves were baffled by all this new technology. When the army purchased its first airplane from the Wright brothers in 1909, the commanding generals—the "top brass"—handed the Wright Military Flyer over to the Army Signal Corps, which put it in with their observation balloons. It never crossed the American military mind that airplanes could be weapons.

Airplanes, when they weren't crashing, proved to be good aerial scouts, and so in July 1914, the army separated the airplanes from the balloons. The new Army Aviation Service had six aircraft. A month later, the Great War—World War I—broke out in Europe. In April 1917, the United States was finally dragged into the war on the side of the British and French Allies. The U.S. generals who hurried to Europe to prepare for the American Expeditionary Force (AEF) scarcely recognized the twentieth-century battlefields. Fragile airplanes had turned into killing machines, branching off into fast "pursuit" fighters and heavy-lifting "bombardment" aircraft. And it wasn't just the airplanes. The ground fighting was unlike anything the Americans generals had ever seen. The stalemated "Western Front" was a continuous line of trenches, hundreds of miles long, stretching from the English Channel to the Swiss Alps. Trench warfare was waged with poison gas, barbed wire, and crawling armored vehicles that the British called "tanks."

The American generals decided that most of their colored regiments were better employed behind the front lines as segregated service units to do the cooking, carrying, and digging. Colored pilots were completely out of the question in 1917. Meantime, Eugene Bullard, an African American boxer who'd enlisted in the French Foreign Legion, was flying combat patrols over the Western Front in a French Spad pursuit aircraft. Bullard was one of two hundred American volunteers already flying in 1917 for the French army as part of its Lafayette Flying Corps. Bullard was also the only one rejected when the other Lafayette pilots, who were all white, transferred to the U.S. Army Air Service. Bullard's example was conveniently overlooked in 1925 when a U.S. Army War College commission declared that segregation was a military necessity based on the "scientific" fact that Negroes were incapable of mastering complex military skills such as piloting.

Rejected by the U.S. Army Air Service, the African American fighter pilot Eugene Bullard continued flying for the French Army until he was grounded by wounds. Recovered, Bullard joined the French infantry and ended World War I as a decorated national hero—a French one.

And yet in 1944, there were African American pilots flying combat in the AAF. John Leahr was one of them. Herb's former classmate from Miss Pitchell's third grade back in Cincinnati had become a Tuskegee Airman. He was one of a handful of black pilots grudgingly trained by the Army Air Corps at a segregated flying school in Tuskegee, Alabama, and sent off to war as a self-contained segregated air force. Everyone in John's Tuskegee squadron was African American, from the cooks to the colonel. Black and white American fliers were allowed to mix only in midair.

In October 1944, Herb knew little about the Tuskegee Airmen beyond what he'd seen in movie newsreels or read in the newspapers. Herb had certainly never trained with black pilots or even flown from the same airfield.

The AAF did its best to make sure that black pilots trained separately, lived separately, and flew separately. Like most white Americans at that time, Herb rarely thought about the problems facing black Americans. In October 1944, Herb had his own problems: he calculated that he had a fair chance of being killed within the next few months somewhere over Nazi-occupied Europe.

Herb knew that his B-17G was bound for the "European Theater of Operations," even if his exact destination was a military secret. "Heavy" bombers like the B-17 were engaged in a dangerous business. American losses were high. In 1944, the figures were still a top secret but on May 7, 1945, when the Germans finally surrendered, the AAF had lost 8,314 heavy bombers in combat. In total, the AAF counted 34,362 killed, 13,708 wounded, and 43,035 missing or captured in European combat operations.

Herb had a good idea of the odds facing him in 1944, top secret or not. He knew about "flak," a contraction of the German word *fliegerabwehrkanonen*, which meant "antiaircraft cannons." Flak was what came out of the cannons—twenty-two-pound artillery shells fired straight up to explode at high altitude in hideous blossoms of white-hot metal fragments that sliced through airplane aluminum. Herb knew about the waves of German Luftwaffe fighters, particularly the Focke-Wulf Fw190 interceptors that attacked the B-17 formations head-on, aiming streams of 20-mm cannon shells straight at the pilots' faces. He'd heard about "Big Week" raids where, day after day, hundreds of bombers attacked the same strategic target. Day after day, 20 percent of the planes didn't make it back. Herb's instructors were all combat veterans. They were the lucky ones who'd been rotated home to train new bomber crews after surviving a tour

A present from Uncle Sam? This is airplane #44-6631, the B-17G that Herb signed for in Lincoln, Nebraska, and flew 7,075 miles to Italy. The airplane was fresh from the Boeing factory in unpainted aluminum.

of at least twenty-five bombing missions. The AAF set the tour number at twenty-five missions after calculating that the average life span of a bomber crew was fifteen missions.

Herb listened closely as these B-17 veterans explained how the overall odds were improving in 1944. There were more American bombers and fewer German fighters, they said. The new B-17Gs were better armed against head-on attacks. They also had long-range escorts, P-51 "Mustang" fighters with extra fuel tanks that allowed them to follow the bombers deep into Germany and bring them home again. So many bomber crews were making it through twenty-five missions that the AAF had raised the magic tour number to thirty and then to thirty-five missions. Overall odds were out of your control, the B-17 veterans told Herb, along with bad weather, bad flak, and bad targets. Your personal odds depended on a well-prepared and well-flown B-17, the instructors said. That depended on your crew. And the crew depended on you, the pilot and commander.

So as the eastern sky over Nebraska finally began to lighten on October 12, 1944, Herb counted heads. His crew was "all present and correct." The aircrew flagged down a canvas-topped army truck to run them out to the flight line. A fuel tanker was topping up the B-17's wing tanks as they arrived. The ground crew chief saluted Herb. The chief's men were

Herb was not only the pilot but the commander of his B-17, in charge of the other nine crew members, both in the air and on the ground. The "duties and responsibilities of the airplane commander" were set out in his B-17 pilot's training manual.

DUTIES AND RESPONSIBILITIES OF

THE AIRPLANE COMMANDER

positioning firefighting carts, wedging wooden chocks under the big landing gear wheels to keep the B-17 from creeping forward during engine start-up, and "spinning the props" by muscle power. The chief's men put their shoulders to the propeller blades and slowly walked them around, spreading the oil inside the cylinders of the giant Wright Cyclone radials before start-up.

Herb's men piled out of the truck, forming a line to relay their duffel bags aboard and stuff them into the B-17G's empty bomb racks. They would fly across the wide Atlantic without bombs or much ammunition but with every gallon of fuel they could carry. Herb's men worked quickly, knowing that each had a preflight checklist to finish before takeoff, but his crew was plainly in good spirits, cracking jokes. They were eager to get going.

As the pilot, Herb began his duties outside the aircraft, scooting underneath with a flashlight to check the "control surfaces"—the flaps, tabs, elevators, ailerons, and tail rudder that steered the great plane through the sky. By 1944 standards, the B-17G was huge, 103 feet from wingtip to wingtip and 75 feet from nose to tail. Empty, the bomber weighed 35,000 pounds. Fully manned, fueled, and armed, it weighed 65,000 pounds. The B-17G was fast for a big bomber—reaching 287 miles per hour. (A modern Boeing bomber, the B-1B Lancer, can reach 1,329 mph at 60,000 feet, carrying weapons that weigh as much as two fully loaded B-17s. A Lancer also costs roughly $283 million.)

Driven by its four twelve-foot propellers, the B-17G could cruise at 30,000 feet, carrying 6,000 pounds of bombs, thirteen heavy machine guns, and a crew of ten. Herb ran his hand over its unpainted aluminum skin and smiled to himself. Once airborne, B-17G number 44-6631 would meet the sunrise in a blaze of flashing aluminum. This was no trainer.

Everyone in Herb's crew was sick of training. This morning, it would end. In the army's alphabet soup of names, Lincoln Field was a POM depot, a Preparation for Overseas Movement center that matched new airplanes to new crews. The moment the B-17G's wheels lifted off the runway at Lincoln, the crew would officially be transferred from a Training command to a Transport command. Crossing the Atlantic, they would transfer from Transport to an Operations command and be assigned to a bomb squadron within a bombardment group within an air force within the Army Air Forces. As the AAF alphabet indicated, there were many air forces. The big question for Herb was *which* air force? Would they go to the legendary Eighth Air Force in England or the newly formed Fifteenth Air Force in Italy? Wherever they were bound, Herb and his crew were still under a Training command until takeoff. No one said a word, but everyone knew how easily the AAF could yank the rug out from under them. A jeep could come roaring out of the shadows with new orders. The control tower could radio with a changed weather forecast, grounding them until further notice in Nebraska.

Army orders changed without warning. The AAF alone had roughly 2.25 million men and women under its command. It flew 60,000 aircraft at home and in half a dozen "theaters" of war around the world, from the Aleutian Islands in Alaska to the Himalayan Mountains in India. And all of it was organized without electronic computers. (The first American electronic computer, the ENIAC, which weighed twenty-seven tons and ran on 17,648 vacuum tubes, was being built in a top secret government laboratory in 1944. One hundred feet long, ENIAC had the same computing capacity as a modern silicon chip two-tenths of an inch square.) The AAF fought World War II with paper and typewriters—mountains of paper and battalions of typists. Whenever the AAF made plans or changed them, the typewriters went into action, and there was no arguing with orders.

The AAF had certainly drilled that into Herb's head. After all, this was his second crew. He had taken his first crew through three months of intensive B-17 Combat Crew Training. They had finished with top marks, but on the day they were to ship out for a POM depot, only nine men reported for duty. One of Herb's waist gunners was AWOL—absent without leave. Being AWOL was serious enough, but the gunner was absent *while under movement orders.* Under military law, that made him a "deserter in the face of the enemy," a grave offense. When the waist gunner turned up later that day, Herb had him arrested by Military Police before his furious engineer could beat him to a pulp. But it was too late. Herb's entire crew had missed "movement." The Training command broke them up, dealing them out one by one to fill gaps in combat-ready crews. As a commander without a crew, Herb was sent back to Combat Crew Training to start all over.

Then Herb got lucky, twice. Instead of starting over, Herb was assigned a crew that had lost its pilot a month into training. But it was awkward. Herb didn't know what had happened to their original pilot. The crew didn't know what had happened to Herb's original crew. The men treated Herb with military courtesy but little confidence until the first night they flew a cross-country training exercise. The training script included an "emergency" landing on a rough airstrip in South Dakota designed for fighter planes. Herb got lucky again, "greasing" the landing—setting the B-17 trainer down on the grass and in the dark with scarcely a bump. Herb knew that a greased landing was more luck than skill, especially at night. But when Herb glanced across the cockpit, his copilot, Harry Poe, was looking back with new respect. After that, the other men had no doubts. They were Herb's crew. But they would stay his crew only if Herb could get their B-17G out of Nebraska before the Training command changed its mind.

It was hard not to rush the preflight check. After all, this B-17G was a brand-new airplane. But learning to fly is learning routines until the routines become habits and learning habits until they become reflexes. Herb was taught to inspect the wings of his Basic trainer so he would always inspect the wings of his B-17G. Only when he'd made a careful circuit around and under his parked aircraft did Herb hoist himself aboard through a small hatch in the nose. Inside, he squeezed behind the bombardier and navigator, busy with their own preflight checks, to reach the flight deck. He slipped into the left-hand seat, the pilot's position, and behind the wheel of his new B-17G.

The "wheel" was actually half a wheel, as if the top had been sawn off, leaving the pilot with a half-moon, three spokes and a hub bearing the Boeing Company nameplate. The steering wheel of an airplane is not like the steering wheel of a car. A car drives in two dimensions; an airplane flies in three. Turning the Boeing's wheel in flight caused the wings (and the B-17) to roll from side to side. Pulling or pushing on the wheel moved the control column, the "stick" that pitched the nose up or down. Herb's heavy flight boots rested on two oversize rudder pedals that turned or "yawed" the plane left or right. Above the rudders were pedals for the parking brakes.

Across the cockpit, his copilot, Harry, had an identical set of controls. On a console between them were the hand controls for the engines and propellers. Herb worked the throttles and propeller pitch–control levers right-handed. Harry worked them left-handed. Between them, pilot and copilot had everything within arm's reach to fly a B-17G.

After putting on his headphones, Herb clicked through the aircraft's "interphone" channels. He could hear his men chattering through their pre-flight checks of radio codes, gun turret motors, high-altitude oxygen masks, fuel tanks, and magnetic deviations. Everything sounded routine. They could be preparing for another training exercise.

Herb started down his own checklist script, ticking each entry off to himself. Takeoff weight and balance report? Check. Controls? Herb signaled to the ground chief outside for visual confirmation as he turned the wheel, pulled back on the control stick, and pumped the rudder pedals. The chief waved as ailerons, elevators, and rudder all responded to Herb's touch. From the copilot's seat, Harry repeated the visual controls check for his side. Fuel transfer valves switched off? "Check," said Harry. Gyroscopes uncaged? "Check." And so Herb and Harry went, checking fuel valves, cowl flaps, throttles, idle cutoff, autopilot, cabin heat, de-icers and anti-icers, right to the bottom of the "Before Starting" list. Next was "Starting Engines."

They began with engine number one, the outboard engine on the pilot's left wing. They would start one engine at a time until they had all four running to specifications. Engine Start was dangerous in an aircraft loaded for takeoff with 2,800 gallons of high-octane aviation gasoline. Herb looked out the window to make sure the fire guard was in position, behind and to the right of engine number one. The chief signaled clear. Herb repeated aloud, "Fire guard and clear left." Harry looked out his side and responded, "Clear right."

Master switches? On. Battery switches and inverters? On. Parking brakes? On. Booster pumps, carburetor filters, fuel levels? Check. "Standing by to start number one," said Harry. Herb put his arm out the window, his index finger raised to indicate engine number one. The chief glanced around at his men before returning the sign. Number one clear for start.

"Fire extinguisher selector, select engine number one," Herb said.

"Number one selected," said Harry.

"Prime number one," said the pilot.

"Number one primed," said the copilot.

"Energize number one," said Herb.

"Energizing number one," said Harry.

Number one began turning with a piercing electric whine. Herb counted off twelve seconds and then called, "Mesh number one."

"Meshing number one," said Harry.

Number one coughed and sneezed blue oil smoke. The prop blades jumped. Then all nine cylinders caught and number one roared to life. The prop blades blurred into a solid disk of spinning steel, their yellow tips a golden band. Herb kept his eyes fixed on number one, judging the speed by sight while reaching back one-handed to adjust the throttle. Harry called out gauge readings—oil pressure, fuel pressure, oil temperature, and cylinder head temperatures—and reported no sign of fire.

Harry said he was ready to start number two. "Fire extinguisher selector, select engine number two," Herb called out. And so they ran the list again, top to bottom for number two, and then across to the right wing for number three engine outside the copilot's window and finally number four, the right outboard engine. Harry reported all engine readings and pressures in the normal range.

Herb switched on the intercom for the final crew check. The tail gunner, the two waist gunners, the ball turret gunner, the flight engineer, the radio operator, the navigator, the bombardier, and Harry were all ready. Outside, the chief signaled his men to pull the wheel chocks. Herb moved his feet to the parking brakes. Ground crewmen came scampering out from under the wings with the chocks. Through the pedals, Herb could feel

Off to war: Herb at the controls of his new B-17G, en route from Nebraska to Italy. At low altitudes, Herb could fly bare-armed and without an oxygen mask. In high-altitude combat, Herb would be bundled up against the cold, masked against the thin air, and armored against the flak.

the powerful Cyclone radials straining to go. The chief made a wide circle around the B-17 to avoid the spinning props, taking up station in front of the aircraft before waving Herb out onto the taxiway. Brakes off, the B-17G rolled forward at a slow walking pace.

On the ground, Herb steered with the spinning propellers, turning the B-17G by speeding up the engines on one wing and throttling back the others. The B-17G was a "tail dragger," a three-wheeled airplane that taxied with its nose in the air, its main bulk resting on its two landing gears, enormous wheels that folded down from under the wing into fixed positions. The rest of the B-17G's weight dragged along behind on a small swivel tail wheel.

Herb let the B-17G roll to a stop and then reset the parking brakes for Engine Run-up. Starting with number one, Herb and Harry ran up the high-altitude turbocharger on each engine. No smoke, no fire, the chief signaled from the ground, and he waved them toward the runway. They were no longer his responsibility.

Herb taxied onto the runway and stopped so the navigator could quickly reset the compass to match the runway's heading. Herb did a final check on turbos, gyroscopes, and generators. "Lock the tail wheel," Herb said. "Tail wheel locked," Harry said. Herb eased his right hand, palm up, under the top throttle lever that gave him control of all four engines at once. Ready, Herb looked up at the airfield control tower. A green light winked down at them.

Holding the brakes, Herb opened all four throttles. The propeller blades clawed at the air as engine speed came up. Time to go. Brakes off. The aircraft jumped forward, rapidly building ground speed until, with only a gentle pull on the control stick from Herb, the B-17G flew itself off the ground. The plane rose into the sky. The ten young men on board "B-17 airplane number 44-6631" were gone for war, gone for soldiers, every one.

Herb's flight log recorded the journey. They left Lincoln, Nebraska, bound for Manchester, New Hampshire, but were forced by fog to continue on to Bangor, Maine. From Bangor, they hopped to Gander, Newfoundland, on Canada's stormy Atlantic coast, where they were grounded by fog and storms for ten days. They left Gander with sealed orders and instructions to fly for one hour due east out over the Atlantic. An hour out, Herb tore open the envelope and read out the new course. With the rest of the crew listening in, Herb clicked through on the interphone to give the navigator their new heading—south and east for the Azores islands off the coast of Portugal. Everyone knew instantly their destination. From the Azores, they would go to North Africa and on to the Mediterranean theater of operations. That meant southern Italy and the Fifteenth Air Force. That meant Herb's crew would be joining the strategic bombing campaign against Germany from the south, flying north along the eastern coast of Italy up the long, narrow Adriatic Sea and over the Alps into Austria, Czechoslovakia, and southern Germany. What that would mean to their young lives, no one knew.

Flying through the alphabet: When Herb's B-17 left Nebraska, it moved from an U.S. Army Air Forces training command (AAF badge at left) to a combat command, the Fifteenth Air Force (15th AF badge at right).

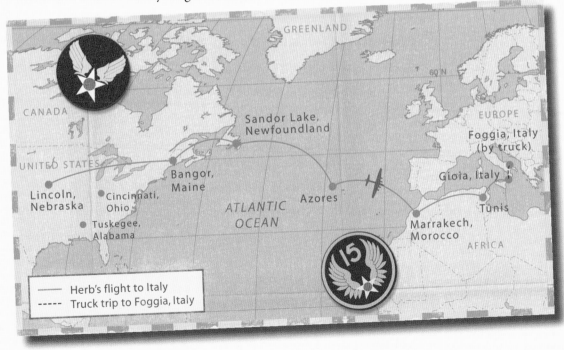

In all, Herb's plane flew 7,075 miles from Lincoln, Nebraska, to Gioia, Italy, covering the distance in forty-one hours in the air but almost four weeks on the calendar because of delays and layovers. Herb, his crew, and the new B-17G arrived at the Fifteenth Air Force headquarters in Italy without a scratch. Their plane was immediately towed away for assignment to a more senior crew. It was no longer "their" airplane. Instead, Herb and his men were bundled into an army truck and bumped along a muddy road to a satellite airfield near the ancient but poverty-stricken village of Lucera. Here Herb and crew joined the 32nd Bomb Squadron of the 301st Bombardment Group. With little ceremony, Herb was assigned a tent, a ground crew, and the next flyable B-17G that the squadron had to spare. Two days later, Herb flew his first bombing mission, riding as copilot with a veteran pilot to get a first look at real war.

★ ★ ★

Herb survived that first combat mission. Over the next five months, he survived thirty-four more, going home in the spring of 1945 without a visible scratch. So did every member of his crew. Only one, a waist gunner, was wounded, hit in the foot by a piece of flak, but he recovered in the base hospital and finished his combat tour safely with another crew. The various B-17Gs that Herb flew in combat didn't do as well. He brought some of them back to Lucera shredded, leaking, and shot up. Herb quickly stopped thinking of any B-17G as "his" plane. He flew what he was given to fly. Once he brought a B-17G back on two engines after the other two gave out over the Alps, hundreds of miles from safety. He set that aircraft down hard on the runway, but everyone walked away from the landing, very glad to be alive. Uncle Sam never asked Herb for the $236,000 back.

Herb could never explain exactly why he survived when so many around him did not. The war kindled a deep religious faith in Herb that stayed with him ever after. Flying in combat, Herb felt he could only put his life into the hands of God and leave it to God to bring him home safely. Death was all around him. He saw friends killed by enemy guns, by accidents, and by bad luck. And yet death passed him by, time after time. The odds were beyond calculation. There were so many close flak bursts, so many near accidents, so many nearly fatal mistakes, and yet Herb survived.

When the war ended, Herb picked up his civilian life again in Cincinnati. Fifty years went by in a flash—marriage, three children, and a successful business career. Then came divorce, remarriage, and a new life with stepchildren and step-grandchildren.

In 1997, Herb read in the Cincinnati paper that the city was honoring the local chapter of the Tuskegee Airmen. Red Tails, Herb remembered. In Italy, the Tuskegees flew red-tailed P-51s when they escorted his squadron. Through the radio chatter over target, Herb remembered hearing the distinctive voices of the Tuskegee Airmen. Unlike other escort fighter groups who couldn't resist tearing off on a wild goose chase after a Luftwaffe decoy, the Red Tails always stayed with the bombers. At the end of the war, it was said that no bomber escorted by the Red Tails was ever lost to enemy fighters. Herb remembered the Red Tails with gratitude and felt that his thanks were overdue.

The mayor was presenting some kind of public award to the Tuskegee pilots on Cincinnati's Fountain Square. Afterward, there was to be a reception in a nearby hotel. Herb invited himself. He went to the hotel reception room where the Tuskegees were milling around, drinks in hand, and cornered the first man he met. Herb explained that he'd been a B-17 pilot in late 1944. Were there any Tuskegee pilots present who'd flown escort missions for the Fifteenth Air Force? That's how Herb met John Leahr for the second time.

Someone pointed John out and Herb cut through the crowd to

introduce himself. Pumping John's hand, Herb announced, "I've been waiting fifty years to meet one of you guys. You saved my tail on many a day." At first, John had no idea what Herb was talking about.

Bit by bit, John Leahr and Herb Heilbrun pieced together their Fifteenth Air Force connection, and as they talked on, they discovered even more in common. The men were both born in 1920, John in May and Herb in October. Both had come up through Cincinnati public schools, and both had started college during the Depression. Both joined the AAF immediately after Pearl Harbor. Both had to wait months to be called into pilot training, so both took jobs at the same airplane engine factory, Wright Aeronautical in Lockland, Ohio. Herb tested engines, firing up GR-2600-655 Cyclones on test stands. John worked in the plant foundry. The work was filthy, hot, and done exclusively by blacks, John told him.

Gradually, John and Herb became friends. They went out to lunch together. They met each other's families and visited each other's homes for dinner. Matching up dates, John and Herb discovered that they had flown together on two missions in 1944: Blechhammer on December 11 and Brux on December 16.

They compared notes on growing up in Cincinnati. As Herb recalled it, "Johnny and I were having dinner, and he said, 'You know, I grew up in North Avondale,' and that's when I said, 'So did I.' And I remember what he said: 'There were only five black families in North Avondale, and I went to a school on Clinton Springs Avenue. It was an old mansion.' And I said, '*I* went to that school. I lived on Warwick right where it came into Clinton Springs, and I would just walk up Warwick and right into school.' Well, then he said, 'I don't remember you.' And I said, 'I don't remember *you.*'"

But Herb had saved nearly everything, including his third grade picture of Miss Pitchell's class. There are forty-two children in the photo with their teacher. They are posed on the steps of the old mansion that housed North Avondale Elementary in 1928. The children are wearing their best outfits for the photographer. There are twenty girls, mostly in short cotton dresses and short 1920s bobbed haircuts. There are twenty-two boys, most in sweaters, a few in jackets and ties. John recalled his first glimpse of the picture. "Herb sent this to me with a little note that said, 'John, this thing is getting crazier and crazier by the minute. If that little black guy in this picture is you, well, that kid behind him who is almost touching him is me.'"

The picture that makes the story: It was long ago, and neither John nor Herb remembered the other until Herb dug up Miss Pitchell's 1928 class picture. That's Herb right behind John.

"So that's me right there," John said, tapping the face of the only black boy in the class. The two men were having lunch in a deli and had pushed back their empty sandwich plates to make room for the photograph. "And that's Herb right there," John said, tapping the white boy with the bangs standing directly behind him.

"And see that black girl there?" said Herb. "I remember her name was Mary Louise Hillman, because my mother's name was Mary Louise Heilbrun."

"That's what Herb told me," said John. "So I said that I was in a class with a black girl, and the only black student I remember was Mary Louise Hillman. So I told Herb, 'If you were in the class with her, then you were in the class with me, 'cause we were both in the same class.' Herb, do you know she's still living right down the street from the school on Clinton Springs? She's not in the same house but she's in the same neighborhood."

"Now, isn't that something?" said Herb, admiring the photo again. "This was 1928. That's a few weeks ago."

In the mirror of time, everything seemed closer to Herb and John than it first appeared. They'd both worked as salesmen. They were both family men, active in church, sports, or community work. And they both remembered their wartime flying vividly. Some veterans who came home from World War II shut their minds and memories tight against what they'd seen. "War is all hell," said the Civil War general William Tecumseh Sherman, and he wasn't kidding. But now as Herb and John became old friends, they wanted to tell strangers about their war, about their struggles to become pilots, and about their friends who didn't come home. They didn't want the air war they'd fought at 30,000 feet to be forgotten. And John especially didn't want the Tuskegees and their separate war against racism to be forgotten. So John and Herb went out on a mission together. They would tell school kids and anyone else who would listen about their long journey from Miss Pitchell's third grade to World War II and home again. Old friends at last, they didn't have any more time to waste.

CHAPTER TWO
Schoolboys

It was called the "color line," and in 1928 it ran everywhere in America. The color line ran through neighborhoods. It ran through schools. It ran through jobs, churches, the U.S. Army, Navy, and the Marines. It ran through professions, cemeteries, railroads, and the balconies of movie theaters. Without warning, the color line could bend or break, and you wouldn't know unless you gave it a push or until you felt it slam shut on your fingers. Sometimes the color line was out in the open, written in law and painted on signs. Usually, it was hidden but there just the same.

One place the color line never crossed was the imagination of John Leahr. In 1928, John's mind was still running overtime from the magical charge it had received the year before. In August of 1927, John could be found running up and down the street in front of his parents' house, wild with excitement. He scanned the sky, shouting every time he spotted an airplane droning high overhead, "Is that him? It's got be him!" And then his older brothers would tell John to pipe down. It wasn't him—it wasn't Colonel Lindbergh. But John was not giving up so easily. He knew that the "Lone

Cincinnati was a modern industrial city built on the older, painful racial border between "slave" and "free" states. In 1920, the year John and Herb were born, artist Frances Farrand Dodge painted this street scene.

Charles Lindbergh poses with "The Spirit of St. Louis," the one-seat monoplane that he flew nonstop across the Atlantic in 1927. Transformed by newspaper accounts into the "Lone Eagle," Lindbergh fired the aviation dreams of "Intrepid Youth" everywhere, including Cincinnati.

Eagle" was coming to Cincinnati that day. The newspapers said so. All the grownups said so. Any minute, John would spot a silver speck in the sky. It would grow larger as the airplane came closer and closer until everyone would realize that this was the most famous airplane in the world, "The Spirit of St. Louis," piloted by "Lucky Lindy," the most famous aviator in the world. Then Colonel Lindbergh would zoom his powerful ship earthward, descending toward Cincinnati's airport, where maybe the mayor and several brass bands were waiting to greet him. To reach the airport, surely the Lone Eagle had to fly right over John's house. Surely the Lone Eagle would stick his head out the cockpit window and wave to the boy running up and down the street below, and then John would shout, "It's him! It's Lucky Lindy!"

To look back from the early twenty-first century to John's and Herb's childhood in the early twentieth century, two things are hard to imagine: first, how difficult the color line made almost everything for African Americans, and second, how crazy all Americans were about airplanes. The color line has a long and tangled history, but the national airplane mania flowed through one man, Charles A. Lindbergh. Throughout the 1920s, American newspapers were full of airplane stories—tragic crashes, daring firsts, combat "aces," and aeronautical innovations—but the newspapers had never seen anything like Lindbergh's nonstop flight from New York to Paris on May 20–21, 1927.

There were no regular news reports on the radio. Radio reporting hadn't been invented yet. Newspapers were still the fastest source for information. It took Lindbergh thirty-three and a half hours to fly the Atlantic in his silver monoplane, "The Spirit of St. Louis." It took the front-page headlines two days to follow him.

Cincinnati Enquirer, Saturday, May 21, 1927:

Lindbergh Is Winging Toward Coast of Ireland;

Passes Newfoundland, Due at Paris at Midnight;

On and On in Darkness,

Gallant Airman, Cruising Alone, Speeds to Meet Rising Sun

Cincinnati Enquirer, Sunday, May 22, 1927

BRAVO, LINDBERGH!

Yankee Airman Arrives in France,

Epic Transatlantic Journey Is Complete in 33 ½ Hours

"Well, Here We Are!" Intrepid Youth Exclaims as He Lands

Amid Delirious Crowd;

Police Line Swept Aside as Thousands Surge onto Field

to Greet American;

A new epoch in aviation has been inaugurated.

The "Intrepid Youth" was actually twenty-five years old when he landed in Paris, but around the world, the hearts of Intrepid Youth took wing. The new epoch flourished in John's mind. Then that August came sensational news: "Lindy is coming," the *Enquirer* announced: "Cincinnati is to see Colonel Lindbergh."

Being seven years old in 1927, John may have missed a few of the finer points of Lindbergh's visit. Lindbergh was not, in fact, coming to Cincinnati in his "Spirit of St. Louis," which had been crated up in Paris and sent safely back to America by ship. The Lone Eagle was piloting a bigger five-seat monoplane so he could take four business associates with him. They were bound for St. Louis, where the financial backers of the "Spirit of St. Louis" were anxiously awaiting the Gallant Airman with parades, banquets, and speeches. Cincinnati was on the way to St. Louis, so Lindy decided to stop there and refuel. There would be no brass bands in Cincinnati, only a fuel truck, a few politicians, and some old friends who knew Lindbergh from his days as one of the first U.S. Air Mail pilots. Lindbergh had made dozens of air mail trips to Cincinnati in 1925, but no one outside the airfield fence took much notice then. Now Lucky Lindy was the most famous man on earth. But when he touched down at Cincinnati's Lunken Field, he stayed close to his airplane as it was refueled, greeting old friends and saying as little as possible to newspaper reporters. Then the Lone Eagle was off again.

The details of Lindy's Cincinnati stop didn't matter to John. He had the main point: the Lone Eagle would fly over Cincinnati and John would be on the lookout, ready to wave. John believed that someday he too would climb into the cockpit of a high-powered airplane and make history in the skies. And while he waited, this Gallant Junior Airman cruised alone, up and down his street, his arms out like wings, ready to meet the rising sun.

★   ★   ★

When John and Herb were boys, the color line was particularly vivid in Cincinnati because the city stood on an older, painful racial border. The Ohio River, which separates Ohio from Kentucky, was the boundary before the Civil War between the Northern "free" states and the Southern "slave" states. Long after the Civil War erased the slavery boundary between North and South, Cincinnati still prided itself on being a city with northern laws but southern racial manners. By 1928, the year John and Herb found themselves together in the third grade, the color line in Cincinnati was invisible in law but razor sharp in daily life.

Down South—that is, south of the Ohio River and down the Mississippi in the states of the old Confederacy—the color line was legal. Segregation was written into local codes called "Jim Crow" laws. The nickname came from a pre–Civil War "blackface" minstrel song in which a happy slave danced around, singing, "Ebr'y time I w[h]eel about and jump Jim Crow." Down South, the Jim Crow laws jumped all over any African American who stepped across the color line.

Jim Crow was de jure, or legal, segregation. But at least you could clearly see Jim Crow segregation down South. Colored schools and facilities were marked. Notices were posted in public places like train stations so a traveler wouldn't confuse "white" and "colored" water fountains, even if the water for them flowed from the same pipe. De jure segregation was also backed up by an even more complicated code of unwritten rules, local traditions, and violent threats. The threats were illegal but real.

Up North, the color line was real, if theoretically illegal. That was de facto segregation, or segregation as a fact of life. In 1928 Cincinnati, de facto segregation ran without wall signs or Jim Crow laws, but a de facto color line

It's early Saturday morning, and these boys, waiting for the Cincinnati public library to open, are "pages," helpers hired to take books by streetcar from the central library to their neighborhood branches. Neither John nor Herb is in this picture, but it shows how nearly all boys dressed at the time: short jackets, knee-length "knickerbocker" trousers, high woolen socks, ankle boots, and cloth "newsboy" caps.

could be as hard to break as any public law down South. In Cincinnati, African Americans could legally drink from any public water fountain. They could vote (and Ohio blacks still tended to vote Republican, the party of Lincoln). They could sit anywhere on a Cincinnati streetcar, but when they got off at their home stop, they would most likely be in a "colored" neighborhood. De facto segregation also ensured that there were colored restaurants, colored library branches, and colored jobs. Newspaper classified ads in the *Enquirer* didn't beat around the bush in 1928: "A few of our Wants: Cooks, second (shift), also fry $125 a month; Cooks, colored; $90 mo(nth)." Growing up in Cincinnati, African American children quickly learned which corner storekeepers would not serve them, which department stores would not allow their mothers to try on clothing, and which movie houses would not sell their parents a ticket or would make them sit in the colored balcony.

The most visible sign of de facto segregation was in school. The Ohio legislature had outlawed separate "colored" schools in 1884. Yet in 1928 Cincinnati, colored children from colored neighborhoods went to colored neighborhood schools (even if they sometimes had to walk past white schools to get there). African American teachers could teach only in colored schools and only at the elementary level. No white child could be taught by a colored teacher.

So how did Herb and John end up standing side by side in Miss Pitchell's class portrait in 1928? The answer is money. Keeping the color line intact was costly, and, sometimes, a little bit of de facto integration could be cost-effective. As things were, the school board could barely keep up with the flood of white children pouring into the neighborhood. Cincinnati's suburbs were booming in the

The founder: John Leahr's great-grandfather, George Carpenter, was a Civil War veteran who bought a few acres in the 1890s on the edge of Cincinnati. The city's white suburbs grew out to surround Carpenter's small enclave of African American families on Clinton Springs Avenue.

1920s, with new streets and new houses going up everywhere. As the original suburb of Avondale filled up, developers moved north on Reading Road and started building North Avondale. The new area, however, wasn't empty. It had been home for decades to the great estates of the city's richest industrial families. By the 1920s, some of these older estates were being carved up for real estate developments and, without land, their once grand mansion houses were sold off cheaply. The school board bought one of these orphans, a "Renaissance Chateau–style" great house at the crest of Clinton Springs Avenue. It was an inexpensive way for the school board to get a large building for a small elementary school. Nearly all the newcomers to North Avondale were white, like Herb Heilbrun's family. A handful of old-timers in North Avondale were black, like John Leahr's family.

George Carpenter, John's great-grandfather on his mother's side, was an African American veteran of the Union army who came to Cincinnati from Virginia. Around 1890, George Carpenter purchased a half-dozen acres of worn-out pasture halfway up Clinton Springs Avenue. At the top of this very steep road were rows of grand mansions. At the bottom were commercial milk dairies. In between was the homestead of George and Elsie Carpenter. Hillside pastures surrounded them, filled with milking cows and milk wagon horses. In the days before refrigerated trucks, it was easier to keep milking cows in the city than it was to bring in fresh milk from the country. No one could imagine how milk could be delivered without horses.

On his land, George Carpenter kept a heavy wagon, a team of horses, and a big scale for weighing the coal he delivered. He also had space to raise vegetables, chickens, and children. It was a good location. True to its name, Clinton Springs Avenue had good water underfoot, and the well George

His great-grandfather George died shortly before John was born, but he remembered his great-grandmother, Elsie Carpenter.

The daughter of George and Elsie, Grace Carpenter Bradshaw was John's grandmother and the undisputed matriarch of Clinton Springs Avenue.

Carpenter sank there never failed. Over the years, George Carpenter subdivided his land for his children and his grandchildren, and for other black families to build their own small houses around him. Many of his new neighbors were servants in the great houses at the top of Clinton Springs Avenue. Carpenter's piece was the only land in miles for sale to blacks. When John's father, Robert Leahr, married John's mother, Rosezelia Bradshaw, it was her mother, Grace Carpenter Bradshaw, who gave the newlyweds a piece of the Carpenter land for a house.

The Leahrs were from Kentucky and, as an outsider, John's father never felt completely at ease living in the shadow of so many Carpenters and Bradshaws. Robert Leahr was a man of great energy and infinite manual skill. While John was a boy, his father was a chauffeur who did all his own maintenance and repairs. Later on, his father repaired furniture, worked in an airplane factory, and retired, at the end of a very long working life, from a Cleveland hospital where he'd mastered the art of setting plaster casts on broken arms and legs.

The dairy cows had been moved to the country by the time George Carpenter's great-grandson John Leahr came along in 1920. Motor trucks brought the milk to town to be bottled, but horse-drawn wagons still delivered it. His great-grandfather had died before John was born, but the Carpenter landholding remained a thriving African American rural enclave of half a dozen families in what was fast becoming suburban North Avondale. Their immediate neighbors were milk wagon horses, so no one objected.

Growing up in their little neighborhood off Clinton Springs Avenue, John and his older brothers, George and Richard, were best friends. It was Richard who nearly got John killed. Richard built a coasting wagon out of wooden planks and a set of cast-off wheels, all steered by a rope tied to the front axle. The lane that ran back from Clinton Springs Avenue was their private racetrack, but out on the main road, traffic was unpredictable. Nonetheless, Richard loaded John between his legs and went shooting down the lane onto Clinton Springs. On the third or fourth run, they shot out into the path of a car. Richard swerved. The car swerved. When the dust cleared, John was lying in the road, bleeding profusely. His right leg was cut nearly to the bone. At the city hospital, the surgeon stopped the bleeding and closed the wound, but as he was discharging John, the doctor took his father aside to say that he wasn't certain that it would heal. If the leg became infected, it might have to be amputated. Hearing that, John resolved to hang on to his leg. He would build it up by running—running to school, running to the store on errands, running everywhere. Whether or not it was the running, his injury healed, but John was left with a long, ugly scar and something wrong with the nerves in his right leg. He'd lost most of the feeling. John also found it hard to balance on that leg. That would come back to haunt him.

The Heilbruns were among the prosperous newcomers to the neighborhood. Herb was an only child, and his parents showered him with affection, as well as toys, clothes, and amusements.

John's oldest brother, George, had been the one to desegregate North Avondale Elementary. When the school opened, George walked up the long hill and was registered. There were no school buses then and the nearest "colored" school was miles away. When Richard was old enough, George took him along up the hill and Richard was registered. There were never more than eight or nine African American children in with the three hundred or so white children at North Avondale Elementary. When John started first grade at North Avondale, three of the nine were Leahrs. The school board left well enough alone at North Avondale Elementary. Sometimes segregation was more trouble than it was worth.

★　★　★

The Heilbruns were among the many newcomers to North Avondale. They were far more prosperous than the Leahrs. John was one of nine children in his family. Herb Heilbrun was an only child. His father was also named Herb, with the usual confusion between senior and junior supposedly prevented by having different middle names. (The young Herb was Herbert Manning Heilbrun; his father was Herbert Leon Heilbrun.) Herb's mother was Mary Louise Louewenstein, a petite, extremely pretty woman who, according to the family story, had a promising tryout during Hollywood's "silent" era but decided that life in the movies was no life at all after she worked several grueling days as a film extra. The Heilbruns rented the ground floor of a new two-family house in North Avondale, but they always had two cars, usually late-model Buicks. Herb's father needed his Buick for long road trips to see his customers all over the Midwest. Herb's mom needed her Buick for when his father was traveling. Women drivers were rare in the 1920s, and women drivers who had their own car were rarer still. Herb's father had married into his mother's family business—a tailoring factory that produced high-quality made-to-measure men's suits. But both sides of Herb's mother's family were wealthy (the other side owned a meatpacking plant), and Herb's father always complained that his in-laws never let him forget that for a minute.

The Heilbruns were Jewish, although Herb's parents were never religious. They didn't belong to a synagogue and never pushed Herb into Hebrew classes or a bar mitzvah at thirteen. Many Jewish families in North Avondale had the same attitude. Being Jewish was an ethnic label. Being religious was their own concern. North Avondale rapidly became a Jewish neighborhood, even if not everyone there was Jewish. Most of the kids at North Avondale Elementary School were Jewish, at least the white kids, because Catholic kids usually went to the Catholic parochial school. The black kids who trudged up Clinton Springs Avenue were mostly Baptists.

Such a mixture could be trouble. In the 1920s and 1930s, America was a lot less tolerant of ethnic and religious differences. Along with the color line, there were other lines that separated "Native Americans" (which in those days meant native-born white Protestants of English-Scottish heritage) from "foreigners" or those of foreign "stock." Like the color line, the ethnic line was usually not out in the open but everyone knew it was there. Help Wanted signs would specify "No Irish." Legal language in real estate deeds would restrict sales to white Protestants only.

American English had a wide and nasty vocabulary to describe all the kinds of Americans who needed to stay on the other side of the line. Any eight-year-old boy playing on the street in 1928 would know a long list of ethnic, racial, and religious derogatory terms. It started with "niggers" and "Injuns" (that is, Native American tribal people who were known in Cincinnati only from cowboy movies) and worked its way through virtually all ethnic groups, including "Krauts," "spics," "guineas," "Polacks," "frogs," "bohunks," "micks," "Japs," "Chinks," and "kikes." When it came to nasty ethnic slurs, Americans were never short of words.

On the streets of Cincinnati, Herb certainly heard all the nasty words for Jews, but it was not until he was inducted into the army in 1943 that Herb was forced to think about his religion. He certainly believed in God, but when the army clerk demanded an answer for the question "Religion?" Herb was confused. What religion did he belong to? The army clerk wasn't waiting long for an answer. The army issued everyone "dog tags," metal identification plates that soldiers had to wear around their neck. The dog tags had a space for "religion" and the army clerk had to put something in that space. "U" for "undecided" was not allowed. So Herb found himself with a dog tag stamped "H" for "Hebrew." When Herb arrived at bomber pilot training school, his buddies told him to get new dog tags. The rumor was that

Herb dressed as a junior airman (top) with leather helmet, coat, and high-top aviator boots. With the family in the tailoring business, Herb was also a well-dressed teenager.

the Nazis were shooting any Jewish pilot who fell into their hands. The story was that somewhere on the base was a sergeant who had a machine that could fix it up, but Herb was such a straight arrow that he never considered altering government records—his dog tags. The army ran on rumors like that, but this rumor turned out to be partly true. The partly true part was awful enough. Toward the end of the war, special Nazi military units went through groups of newly captured American soldiers, pulling out those that they thought were Jews and sending them to slave labor and concentration camps. But these Nazi racial experts paid no attention to dog tags. They'd been trained in Nazi racial "science" to identify Jews. More than half of the two hundred American prisoners of war that they singled out as Jews were not.

In 1928, ugly words were better left outside the third grade at North Avondale Elementary. Both John and Herb remembered being on their best behavior in Miss Pitchell's class. They remembered the May Day festivities at North Avondale Elementary. Wearing costumes, the children danced in opposite circles, weaving the ends of long ribbons fastened to the top around a tall Maypole. John remembered the year all the children were sent home with instructions to come to the Maypole dance dressed as "white snowdrops." Every attic on Clinton Springs Avenue was ransacked for old dresses, coats, and feathers to outfit the little ones for spring. On May Day morning, the black parents marched their white snowdrops up the hill to dance around the Maypole

The "white snowdrops" of Clinton Springs Avenue, decked out for the May Day celebration at North Avondale School. Wearing a regular hat and keeping a straight face in the back row is John's father, Robert Leahr. Wearing a woman's "cloche" cap and standing directly in front of his father is John, with his brother George to the left and brother Richard to the right. Wearing plumes in the front row is Mary Louise Hillman. The little boy is John's brother Bill, and next to him is John's sister Grace.

with their white classmates, trying hard not to laugh at what was for the grownups one of the funniest jokes they'd ever heard about the color line.

In the fourth grade, Herb and John were in different classes. They soon forgot about each other, but they never forgot what it was like being a boy in North Avondale in the late 1920s. They both remembered being wild for airplanes and for airplane stories.

Herb built model airplanes with his best friend and next-door neighbor, Donald Berning. There were two kinds: model airplanes you built to admire and model airplanes you built to fly. Herb liked the first kind, kits of solid wood that he carved, sanded, glued, and painted to look like the real Spad and Fokker biplanes that tangled over the Western Front during the Great War. Donald liked the second kind. The parts came printed on thin sheets of balsa wood that Donald carefully cut out with a razor blade, glued onto spars, and covered with tissue paper. Rubber-band motors drove the models in flight. The work was too painstaking for Herb, but Donald became one of the city's best flying model builders.

Printed on cheap wood pulp paper with lurid color covers, the "pulps" were filled with exciting, violent, and unrealistic stories about gallant airmen dueling over the Western Front during the Great War. Teachers, librarians, and guardians of morality hated pulp magazines. John and Herb loved them.

When they were younger, Herb and Donald tried a more direct approach to flying. They took turns jumping off Herb's front porch, launching themselves into the air from the brick columns on either side of the steps. Then Herb got the idea of having his picture taken in midair and "borrowed" his parents' Brownie box camera. He and Donald worked on that for days. Fortunately, they never broke anything. Unfortunately, Herb never got a picture of himself flying.

Model airplane kits cost money, so John did most of his flying in his mind, reading the "pulps"—story magazines printed on cheap pulp paper that featured sensational tales of adventure, mystery, and aviation. John's favorite pulps were the air combat stories—"Sky

Fighters," "Sky Aces," "Aces," and "G-8 and His Battle Aces"—especially their colorful, violent, and slightly shocking covers. Pulps were cheap—they cost a dime in the 1920s—but whenever a copy turned up on Clinton Springs Avenue, it would stay there forever. John remembered them being passed from hand to hand until the shocking covers fell off.

Inside, the pulp "air combat" stories ran to thousands of words, with titles like "Ace of Doom" and "Death's Double." The great aces were described as "knights of the air" who fought a romantic, almost private war high above the Western Front by a strict code of honor. The pulps were no preparation for aerial combat 30,000 feet over Germany, yet the air stories had a lot to do with John ending up in the cockpit of a P-51. The pulps kept alive John's dreams of flying.

John grew up in a different North Avondale from Herb. In 1928, John knew that black kids were not allowed onto local ball fields, in certain stores, or in any of the local theaters. To see a movie, John had to walk over to the established black commercial district in Walnut Hills. It was an exciting place to visit for an African American boy who lived on a black island in a white suburb. In Walnut Hills, the theaters, restaurants, and stores craved black customers. The crowds on the street were black. The clerks in stores were black. The music coming out of the bars and record stores was black jazz. The only color that counted in Walnut Hills was the color of money.

After John's fifth-grade year, his father announced that the family was moving to Walnut Hills. Perhaps it was the racial isolation of North Avondale. Perhaps it was the strain of living surrounded by his wife's extended family, but his father rented an apartment in Walnut Hills and John transferred to the "colored" elementary there. The move was not a total break from Clinton Springs Avenue for John. He walked back to his old neighborhood regularly to stay with Grandma Bradshaw, to play with old friends, and to tag along with Richard and George on crazy adventures. But he never lived in North Avondale again.

John soon forgot most of his classmates at North Avondale, including a white boy named Herb, who in turn forgot all about a black kid in his class named John. After all, other than the third grade, what else did they have in common? It turned out that when John and Herb were in the third grade, they both wanted to be rich, to be great athletes, to drive the fastest cars, and to fly.

That would be enough in the long run.

In the late 1930s, only a few African Americans could afford the expense or overcome the prejudice of flying schools. This 1937 cartoon by Charles Haywood kept the dream alive for a new generation raised on Lucky Lindy and air pulps.

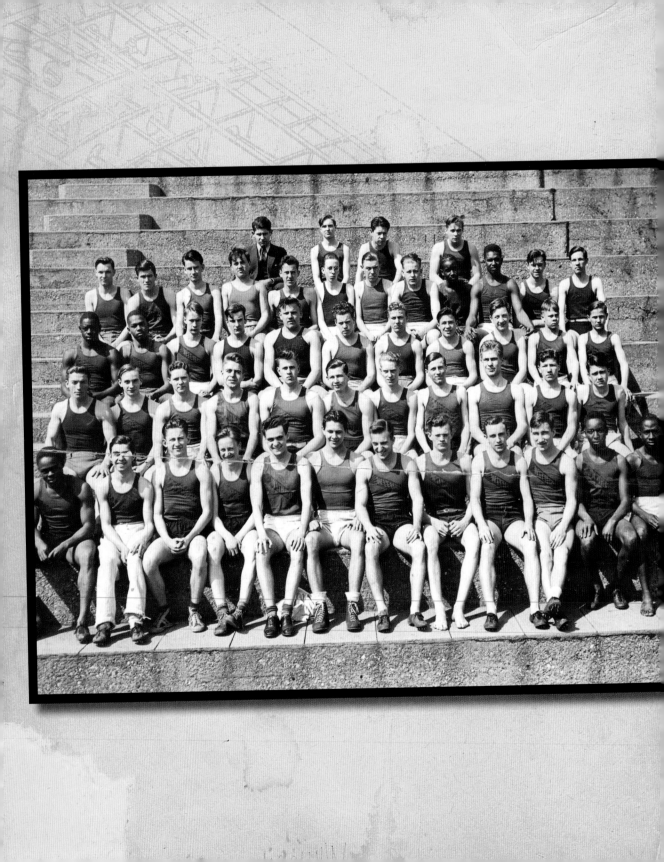

CHAPTER THREE
Volunteers

It seems that every generation has a new terrible date to remember. It's burned into the minds of anyone old enough to remember anything of the day. It becomes the question that ties those who remember it together: "Where you were when the World Trade Center towers fell in 2001?" "Where were you when the space shuttle *Challenger* exploded in 1986?" "Where were you when President Kennedy was assassinated in 1963?" Eventually all these terrible dates pass out of living memory—that is, there is no one still alive who was alive then. The date of April 14, 1865, and the question, "Where were you when you heard that Abraham Lincoln had been shot?" has passed out of living memory. In the early twenty-first century, the date of December 7, 1941, is moving toward the edge. Unless human life span increases dramatically, every terrible date will pass out of living memory in a little over a century. So one day will Pearl Harbor and the entire Second World War. One day, so will September 11, 2001.

December 7, 1941, was a Sunday. In Hawaii, the U.S. Pacific Fleet was anchored with peacetime precision in its home port of Pearl Harbor

Facing a medical rejection because of his old leg injury, John persuaded the army doctor to pass him based on his record with the Withrow High School track team. John (third row, second from left) did run track at Withrow. He just never won a race because of his leg.

A date burned in living memory, December 7, 1941: An enormous fireball erupts from "Battleship Row" as Japanese bombers score hit after hit on the American warships tied up on a peaceful Sunday morning in Pearl Harbor.

when the first wave of Japanese fighters and bombers appeared overhead just before eight a.m. The Imperial Japanese Navy attack planes were launched from aircraft carriers far over the western horizon and reached Pearl Harbor that sleepy Sunday morning undetected and unopposed. Eastern U.S. time is five hours ahead of Hawaiian time, so that made it one p.m. in Ohio when the first bombs and torpedoes began raining down on the great American warships tied up helplessly, side by side, along "Battleship Row."

Herb didn't hear the news until later that afternoon when he stopped on his way home at the Sugar N Spice, a neighborhood restaurant. Herb, who'd turned twenty-one that October, was working at Wright Aeronautical, a sprawling "defense plant" newly opened on the highway north of Cincinnati. Wright Aero made high-powered engines for army medium bombers, and Herb helped test them. The American airplane engine business was booming in late 1941. A new world war was already raging in Europe and Asia, but the United States was officially at peace on that Sunday morning. The U.S. government, however, wasn't sure how long that peace would last. The army was frantic to beef up its air fleet and had placed enough engine orders with Wright Aero to keep Herb and thousands of other newly hired employees working two shifts a day, seven days a week. On December 7, Herb was on the first shift. Between Herb's early breakfast at home and his early dinner at the Sugar N Spice, America was pushed into World War II. When Herb walked into the restaurant, the waitresses, cooks, and customers were hungry only for war news. The "Japs" are bombing Hawaii, they told Herb. The news was on the radio.

John was coming out of the "colored" balcony at a downtown Cincinnati movie theater that afternoon. Looking out through the lobby doors, John knew instantly that something terrible was happening. A big fire? A fatal car crash? People rushed past on the sidewalk, their faces tight with worry. Only when John was outside the theater and across Fifth Street in Cincinnati's central Fountain Square could he finally look up and see what all the panic was about. Headlines flowed across an outdoor electric news ticker on the side of the Hotel Gibson. The words barely made sense—"JAPS," "PEARL HARBOR," "BOMBERS," "FIRES," "BATTLESHIPS." Standing beneath the news ticker, perfect strangers asked perfect strangers what they thought it meant. Most thought it meant war.

Next morning, the front page of the *Cincinnati Enquirer* shouted:

AMERICAN BATTLESHIP REPORTED SUNK
ANOTHER IS SET AFIRE IN JAP ATTACK
Roosevelt to Address Congress Today
War Declared by Tokyo
Heavy Losses Suffered by Army and Navy, Roosevelt Reveals

If the world picture on December 8, 1941, was grim, the personal picture was both scary and exciting for Herb and John. Unmarried, patriotic, and crazy about airplanes, they both knew that pilots were going to be needed in unimaginable numbers. Duty called, but so did adventure. Within days, the Army Air Corps was asking for volunteers with good health, good vision, and the equivalent of two years of college to enlist as aviation cadets. (The education requirements could be met partially by examinations.) John and

Herb came to the same conclusion within weeks of Pearl Harbor. Join the Army Air Corps. Learn to fly. (Officially the Army Air Corps had become part of the new Army Air Forces in June 1941, but the names were used interchangeably well into 1943.)

In January, John went downtown to the federal building to sign up as an aviation cadet. The first hurdle was the regular army physical. John's flying career nearly ended right there. The army doctor wanted a closer look at the leg John had injured as a boy. The long, ugly scar on his right leg was impossible to miss, so John told him the whole story—the coaster car accident, the surgery, and his "run everywhere" recovery plan. The doctor examined his legs and then asked John to stand on one foot and balance. This was always a difficult move for John. John tried his best, but each time he fell over.

On the home front, the Tuskegee Airmen were promoted as symbols of African American courage. On the fighting front, the Tuskegees were shunned by white squadrons and left to learn the painful lessons of air combat survival on their own.

Keep us flying!

BUY WAR BONDS

John knew that he would have to talk his way into the army, and quickly. Otherwise, the doctor would give him an unfit 4-F. Even in the patriotic fervor after Pearl Harbor, many men would have grabbed a 4-F classification and gone dancing out the door. The army was never a tender employer, and its reputation among black men was worse. But John was determined to serve his country and determined to fly. As John remembered it, he grabbed for any story that might change the army doctor's mind. "Honest, Doc, the leg works fine," John pleaded. Then inspiration hit him. "I was on the track team for four years at Withrow High School. I can show you my team picture." What John did not tell the doctor was that in his four years on the Withrow track team, he'd never won a race. Maybe it was John's enthusiasm or maybe it was nearly lunchtime, but the army doctor passed him as fit. Now all John had to do was to present his application to the Army Air Corps, pass a written examination, and be approved by the Cadet Examining Board.

At least John knew that the Air Corps now had to take his application seriously. An Air Corps recruiting officer would have laughed him or any other black volunteer out of his office only a few years before. In early 1942, the first class of Negro pilots had just begun training at the Air Corps' segregated flight school near the Tuskegee Institute in Alabama. Like most African Americans in the 1940s, John knew about the Tuskegee flight program because of the "Negro press," weekly newspapers that provided the only serious coverage of blacks in politics, in the arts, and in the armed services. The white press usually ignored Negro news, unless it was crime news.

Before Pearl Harbor, the Negro press had been angrily debating how and even whether African Americans should support a future American war. After Pearl Harbor, the Negro press rallied to the flag by endorsing the "Double V for Victory" campaign, which was originally proposed by the writer James G. Thompson. He took the British war slogan "V for Victory," which meant victory over the Axis powers, and doubled it for victory over racism in the United States as well. Thompson declared, "The 'V for Victory' sign is being displayed prominently in all so-called democratic countries which are fighting for victory over aggression, slavery, and tyranny. If this V sign means that to those now engaged in this great conflict, then let colored Americans adopt the double VV for a double victory. The first for victory over our enemies from without, the second V for victory over our enemies within."

Roy Wilkins, editor of the *Crisis* magazine, published by the National Association for the Advancement of Colored People (NAACP), agreed. Black

Americans had special war aims, Wilkins wrote: "Though thirteen million American Negroes have more often than not been denied democracy, they are American citizens and will in every war give unqualified support to the protection of their country. At the same time, we shall not abate one iota our struggle for full citizenship rights here in the United States. We will fight, but we demand the right to fight as equals in every branch of the military, naval, and aviation service."

All this talk of racial equality filled the Air Corps' top command with dread. But it was too late in 1942 to stop black military aviation completely. In 1938, the Air Corps had made a tactical error while negotiating with Congress over a new civilian pilot training program. That error opened a tiny crack in its "white pilots only" policy. But the Air Corps had been desperate in 1938, desperate for new warplanes and desperate for time to train new pilots to fly them.

Flying an airplane is not a natural talent. You need certain natural abilities—good vision and good reflexes—plus a good basic education to train as a military pilot, but learning to fly *well* is also a matter of time. The Air Corps measured the time needed in flying hours. If you were a rookie pilot, the Air Corps figured you needed at least two hundred flying hours before you could move on to another one hundred flying hours in combat training. Once in air combat, you were a rookie all over again. Gaining combat flying hours was a matter of life or death—*your* life or death. Air war eats rookies.

To gain some of that time, the Air Corps top brass asked Congress in 1938 to pay for a new civilian pilot training program on college campuses. They were so desperate to get the CPTP going, the commanders agreed to include a few traditionally all-black colleges. Yet the Air Corps remained deliberately vague about what it would do with these unwanted black CPTP pilots in the event of war.

The most successful black CPTP program was set up at the Tuskegee

Institute in Alabama. Waiting for the Air Corps at Tuskegee was an African American soldier who knew a tactical error when he saw one. Captain Benjamin O. Davis was a West Point graduate and the commander of the Tuskegee ROTC, one of the army's few black officer-training programs. Captain Davis was the son of Major Benjamin O. Davis, Sr. In 1940, Captain Davis and Major Davis were the only black officers on active service in the U.S. Army.

The Air Corps had turned down a pilot training application from the junior Davis at the end of his senior year at West Point. The rejection was intended as a slap in the face. It was one of many for Davis, the only black cadet at West Point. Davis had been shunned during his four years there by his fellow cadets, who swore not to associate with him. No one would room with Davis. No one would speak to him except in the direct line of duty. Cadet Davis graduated thirty-fifth out of 276 in the West Point Class of 1936. His application to become an army pilot was instantly rejected. After all, the Air Corps "knew" that Negroes couldn't fly. But Davis wasn't done with the Air Corps. When the CPTP opened at Tuskegee in 1940, Captain Davis took note. As a serving army officer, Captain Davis was ineligible for a civilian training program. But he'd spotted the Air Corps' tactical error. West Point had taught Captain Davis how to take advantage of tactical errors.

In January 1941, the Air Corps finally caved to political pressure. As an experiment, the Air Corps announced that it would form a Negro flying unit, the 99th Pursuit Squadron (all pursuit squadrons were later renamed fighter squadrons). For its first black aviation cadet class, the Air Corps said it would take CPTP graduates, "qualified" civilians, and "serving" army personnel. Captain Davis applied at once. Cadets who survived flight school would be trained as fighter pilots for the 99th. Of course, this black fighter squadron existed only on paper in early 1941. The Air Corps brass hoped it would stay on paper. Captain Davis had other ideas.

That a white woman would trust her life to a black pilot was news enough. That the woman was Eleanor Roosevelt, wife of President Franklin D. Roosevelt, was front-page news. Eleanor went flying with "Chief" Anderson at the Tuskegee training field in March 1941.

That spring, Eleanor Roosevelt, the activist wife of President Franklin Delano Roosevelt, visited the CPTP airfield at Tuskegee. All the civilian flight instructors at Tuskegee were black, and Mrs. Roosevelt came right to the point with the top instructor, C. Alfred "Chief" Anderson. "I always heard that Negroes couldn't fly," said Mrs. Roosevelt. "I wondered if you'd mind taking me up." Chief Anderson said he'd be delighted.

Mrs. Roosevelt's Secret Service agents protested. Mrs. Roosevelt brushed them aside and climbed into the back seat of Chief Anderson's Piper "Cub" trainer. A photographer took their picture. Chief Anderson took off, circled the southern Alabama skies for a few minutes, and landed without incident. If you want to know how much America has changed since World War II, consider this famous photograph. It shows a middle-aged white woman smiling cheerfully from the back seat of an airplane about be flown by a young black man. This was front-page news in 1941. Apparently, Negroes could fly.

The Negro press certainly didn't miss the significance of Eleanor's flight. They redoubled their coverage of the Tuskegee CPTP. In July 1941, the Army Air Corps finally accepted its first fifteen colored aviation cadets. Fourteen of the fifteen were CPTP graduates. The fifteenth was Captain Davis.

The attack on Pearl Harbor six months later buffaloed the Air Corps into expanding the Tuskegee program. The Negro press carried the news that the Air Corps would train enough pilots for an all-black, three-squadron fighter group to be designated as the 332nd Fighter Group. Privately, the Air Corps top brass was determined to sidetrack the Tuskegee airmen. Publicly, the door was open. John was determined to get through that door before it slammed shut.

John survived the army physical, the Air Corps qualification exam, and the Cadet Board of Examiners. His Air Corps acceptance letter told him to stand by for call-up to an aviation cadet class at Tuskegee. The delay made John nervous. Until he was sworn in as a cadet, John was just another civilian. He'd already passed the army physical exam and was thus a prime candidate for the draft. In March, the Negro press reported on the graduation of the first Tuskegee class. Of the fifteen who'd entered flight training, only Captain Davis and four others survived to pin on their metal "wings." They became the first African American military pilots in U.S. history.

The Tuskegee program was clearly a narrow doorway. John worried that his cadet call-up would come too late. One by one, the other young men in his neighborhood disappeared into the armed services, either as volunteers or draftees. Despite the "Double V for Victory" talk, military service for most blacks in World War II was the same old segregated story: black units did the same menial work that most segregated black regiments performed in the Great War—digging holes, moving heavy loads, and cleaning up. John's brother George was in the army. Richard was in the navy. John's youngest brother, William, was sent to the army's last segregated cavalry regiment, that is, until their horses were taken away. The last white cavalry units were converted to armor and artillery. William's black cavalry regiment was converted to field engineers. They dug big holes.

Colonel Benjamin O. Davis, Jr. (at left), with his second in command, Edward Gleed, in Italy. Getting to the air war was half the battle for Davis.

John's mom came home steaming mad one afternoon. Some neighborhood busybodies had been wondering aloud when "Cadet John" was going to flying school, and Rosezelia had to set them straight. Meantime, John was reading stories in the Negro press about black men awaiting call-up into the aviation cadets who were being drafted into the regular segregated

John's mother, Rosezelia Leahr, was more worried about her son flying over Jim Crow Alabama during training than over enemy territory in Europe later on. Ironically, the German Luftwaffe refused to segregate captured Tuskegee pilots in their POW camps, despite protests from white AAF officers.

army. The Air Corps was dragging its feet on black aviation, the Negro press grumbled. John saw the color line drawing in tight again, just in time to strangle his hopes.

Herb was also starting to sweat his call-up. In May 1942, Herb passed the Air Corps exams and the Cadet Board of Examiners. Like John, Herb was sent home to wait for a suitable aviation cadet class opening. The odds were better for Herb. For John, it was Tuskegee or nothing. For Herb, the Air Corps had thousands of possible openings in flight schools across the country, yet the months went by and the young men in Herb's neighborhood thinned out.

At least Herb could say to himself that he was performing important war work, testing B-25 bomber engines. Curiously, John and Herb were working in the same place in 1942 without knowing it—Wright Aeronautical. They could have met in the Wright Aero parking lot and talked over old times with Miss Pitchell. Of course, Herb and John probably would not have recognized each other.

The Wright Aero plant outside Cincinnati was a critical part of America's defense buildup. The factory had been hastily built to manufacture the Wright GR-2600 Cyclone, a turbocharged fourteen-cylinder double radial engine intended for the military's most advanced propeller fighters and bombers. In 1940, there were cornfields on the plant site. In late 1942, there were 20,000 people working round the clock at Wright Aero, including Herb and John. It's small wonder that they never met.

The color line is the other reason that they never met at Wright Aero. Herb worked in the testing department. Every GR-2600 was wheeled from the assembly line to Herb's department for "static testing." Its fuel, oil, and controls were connected just as they would be on a B-25. Then, from a control panel a safe distance away, Herb fired it up. The R-2600 roared to life, all 1500 unmuffled horsepower under Herb's control and the scrutiny of his test gauges. It was loud and smoky but exciting work. Everyone who worked in the testing department with Herb was white, except for the janitors.

John worked in the foundry at Wright Aero. Here the men poured molten aluminum into casting molds and "shook out" formed cylinder heads. John's job was to clean up the rough castings, grinding off metal spurs and drilling out the internal passages. The foundry was loud, smoky, and sometimes dangerous. It was always filthy. Everyone who worked in the foundry department with John was black, except for the foremen.

Yet it wasn't that simple. Nothing about the color line was simple. Herb and John had graduated in the same year—1938—from different Cincinnati public high schools. So few black students qualified for college preparatory programs that it was easier to "mix in" a few at white high schools than it was to build a separate colored high school. Withrow High School, where John ran on the track team but never won a race, was another local exception to Cincinnati de facto segregation. At Withrow, blacks were treated with icy politeness, low expectations, and a few special rules. Blacks, for example, could use the swimming pool only on Friday afternoons, after which the water was drained. Herb's high school, Hughes, also had a few colored students sprinkled through its overwhelmingly white student body, but the races lived in parallel worlds.

Their families also had different dreams. John was the first in his family to start high school, let alone to graduate. His mother was determined that John would go as far as his brain could carry him, including college. College for Herb was more like inertia. Herb went to Ohio State University in Columbus, chiefly because his father said he would pay for it. At Ohio State, Herb socialized heavily, studied lightly, and came home with a year of academic credits but little desire to go back. Herb had even less desire to go into the family suit-making business. Herb did odd jobs around his father's office, but his mind was elsewhere. Then Herb was elsewhere—on a cross-country camping trip with friends and then an epic fishing trip to Canada.

When he got back, Herb spotted a newspaper ad that promised an escape from the tailoring business. The ad announced a new technical training course being organized locally by an aircraft company. This outfit, Wright Aero, was going to build a new engine factory near Cincinnati and needed young men with some college background to train as technical engineers. It would be a paid job but the trainees would start in a classroom before graduating to advanced on-the-job training at the plant. Herb would have to pass a serious math exam to get in and a more serious exam to graduate. Herb dug out his barely used college math textbook and, for the first time in his life, he studied. A year later, Herb was applying his book knowledge of pressure and temperature to roaring R-2600 Cyclones in the testing department at Wright Aero. Flying, though, was always the goal, and Herb reasoned that his knowledge of airplane engines would make him an even better pilot. Yet 1942 went by and 1943 began and Herb was still home and still working at Wright Aero and waiting for flight school.

John's path to Wright Aero was also roundabout. His mother was delighted when John announced his intention to become a college man. This was the true Carpenter spirit, she said. John's father was also proud, but his total college support fund came to fifty dollars. John took the cash, caught a ride north to Wilberforce, the nation's oldest private African American college, near Xenia, Ohio, and talked his way into full-time matriculation. He put the fifty dollars toward his tuition and took a job as a waiter in the college dining hall.

John made it through a hectic but exciting year at Wilberforce, studying political science, starring in a touring production of Langston Hughes's play

Don't You Want to Be Free?, and waiting tables in the dining hall. Students ate "family style," eight to ten at the same long table for every meal. Each table had its own waiter, who brought out the food in big bowls and heaping platters to be passed around. It was hard work, hefting the heavy trays and keeping up with his table's demands, but John didn't mind. The waiters ate afterward in the kitchen, and they ate well. More important, waiting tables paid his tuition. But during the spring semester, John found himself butting heads with one of his diners. John couldn't even recall how it started, but this fellow was constantly grumbling about the service and barking orders at him. One evening at the end of term, he accused John of deliberately starting the meat platter at the far end of the table. That turned into a shouting match. Then a shoving match. Friends grabbed John's arms to keep him from worse trouble. The fellow took advantage of John's helplessness to punch him in the eye. John was more surprised than hurt. He shook off his friends and gave the unhappy diner a taste of his own medicine.

The fight made him unemployable at Wilberforce. "I can't have my waiters hitting my customers," said the woman who ran the dining halls. Without a campus job, John had to transfer to the University of Cincinnati, the city's "streetcar" college. Like John, most UC students lived at home, commuted to school by streetcar, and worked odd jobs to cover tuition. John did campus maintenance—mowing, mopping, and trash collection. He also picked up bodies at the city morgue for delivery to medical school anatomy classes. After the excitement of Wilberforce, the city university felt like high school again to John, complete with color line distinctions. Academically, he found himself being plugged back into the colored school system. The city university routinely shunted its few black students into its College of Education. This was considered sound academic advice. Teaching in a colored

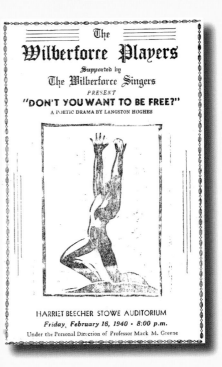

The Wilberforce Players
Supported by
The Wilberforce Singers
PRESENT
"DON'T YOU WANT TO BE FREE?"
A POETIC DRAMA BY LANGSTON HUGHES

HARRIET BEECHER STOWE AUDITORIUM
Friday, February 16, 1940 · 8:00 p.m.
Under the Personal Direction of Professor Mack M. Greene

John played the lead role in this Wilberforce College student production of a play by the African American poet Langston Hughes. Even though John had to work off his tuition as a waiter, he found his freshman year at the all-black Wilberforce a welcome escape from the low expectations that "mixed" schools had for black students.

school was the only real career opportunity for Negroes with college degrees. It infuriated John. He'd wanted to study law or economics, not elementary education. A required children's music course was the final straw. "I just can't stand singing 'Tra la la' at three o'clock in the afternoon," John told his mother when he announced that after finishing one year in elementary education, he couldn't face another. Someone told him that a new defense plant north of town was hiring coloreds. John went along to Wright Aeronautical and was grinding cylinder heads in the foundry on Pearl Harbor Sunday.

His year at the city university along with his year at Wilberforce gave John the two years of college credit needed for the aviation cadets. Yet the months went by at Wright Aero, and John still had no call-up orders. His draft board finally gave John a two-week ultimatum: Get into the Air Corps or get drafted. John watched his mailbox like a hawk. On the last Friday of the ultimatum, John called in sick and drove up to Wright Army Airfield near Dayton, looking for someone in the induction office who would take pity on him. A sympathetic captain told John that if he could pass the induction physical, he could swear John in to the Army Air Corps Enlisted Reserves that afternoon. That would protect John from the draft board. This time, John's teeth—not his injured leg—let him down. Looking into John's mouth, the Air Corps examining physician spotted two visible cavities. The doctor got all huffy. How could he pass a man for pilot training with two great holes in his teeth? What if a toothache flared up at 10,000 feet? John dashed into Dayton to find a dentist who'd see him at once and fill two teeth for the cash he had in his pocket.

John arrived back at Wright Field just before five. The induction office was closing, the desk clerk said, as he tried to shoo John out the door. The sympathetic captain stuck his head out to see who was causing such a ruckus. He saw John. The captain said he was sorry, but there was nothing he could do that day about his physical. Come back on Monday. John opened his mouth and pointed to his sparkling new fillings. As John remembered it, the captain laughed, shook his head, and said, "Raise your right hand . . ." John was in the Air Corps Reserves, just barely.

In November 1942, John was finally called up from the Enlisted Reserves for his cadet training class. Herb sweated it out until February 1943. By then, John was already flying.

CHAPTER FOUR
Cadets

The army for John began in typical army style. John had to buy his own train ticket from Cincinnati north to Columbus, Ohio, to be sworn in as an aviation cadet. There he was handed an army train ticket south to cadet training in Tuskegee, Alabama. The train went through Cincinnati. John was still in his civilian clothes—his civvies—when his southbound train stopped briefly in Cincinnati. John needed no reminder of his hometown's other special racial distinction—railroad segregation began in Cincinnati. As trains left Cincinnati for southern destinations, conductors walked through, telling African American passengers who didn't know Kentucky's Jim Crow civil code that they had to move to the colored car, which was usually the first one behind the smoky, coal-burning locomotive. After Cincinnati, the restaurant car was closed to blacks, although sometimes they could buy food there to take back to their seats in the colored car.

On the ride south toward Cincinnati, John had already moved to what would become the colored car once the train crossed the Ohio River. John was determined to let nothing on his journey into the Deep South jeopardize

A PT-17 roars overhead. Its fragile-looking canvas wings and fuselage were deceptively strong, and the PT-17 was famous for withstanding student pilot abuse.

flight training. In May, he was promoted to Advanced. On July 28, 1943, John was one of twenty-seven survivors out of the original sixty in Class SE 43-G to pin on silver wings. He was commissioned Second Lieutenant J. H. Leahr, United States Army Air Forces. Back home, the *Cincinnati Post* ran his AAF graduation photo. It was a picture to knock your eye out. It showed a clear-eyed young man, an African American pilot, posed with his flying helmet unsnapped, his goggles up on his forehead, his radio earphones unplugged. On his shoulders are officer's bars. In 1943, that was a picture worth a second look.

The week John was getting his wings, Aviation Cadet Heilbrun was flying short cross-country trips across Arizona, navigating from Wickenburg to Thunderbird and then from Thunderbird back to Wickenburg. It was his last week in Primary and his last time in a Stearman PT-17. In August, Herb

would transfer to Pecos, Texas, for Basic flight school. In late September 1943, Herb would get his wings, his officer's bars, and the assignment he'd begged for—multiengine aircraft. Multiengine training meant bombers.

Less than a year before that, Herb's aviation cadet career had been hanging by a thread or, at least, by an x-ray. The army screened all incoming cadets for tuberculosis and one of the doctors at his final induction physical thought there were suspicious spots on Herb's lung x-ray. TB would end Herb's already delayed flying career, so Herb begged the army doctor to contact his own doctor in Cincinnati. Herb's doctor had seen those spots before and decided that they were just "calcification" marks. Herb pleaded. The army doc made the call. Herb's doctor repeated his calcification spots diagnosis. It's nothing, Herb's doctor said. Your x-ray machine must be set at the wrong angle. But, sir, said the army doctor, I can't pass a man for flight school with an x-ray that looks like this. Herb's doctor had a suggestion: Turn Herb's body slightly sideways and reshoot the x-ray. That worked.

There was a war on. Herb didn't want to miss it.

While still in flight school, cadets like John (left) and Herb (right) wore a variety of AAF clothing, from flight suits to full dress uniforms. Aside from insignia, you could always tell an air cadet by his cap. It had a wire sewn into the top brim, giving it a sharp edge. Once out of flight school, full-fledged AAF pilots were allowed to remove the wire inside the hat brim so it wouldn't interfere with their earphones in the cockpit. The result was a shapeless mass that became known as the "fifty mission crush," meaning that your earphone-crushed hat made you look like a war-weary seasoned combat vet. A good "crush" was the height of AAF fashion.

CHAPTER FIVE

Fighters

In the Great War, one-on-one aerial combat was called "dogfighting" and the name stuck. But the image of two snarling canines circling each other for the kill didn't fit the dogfights of World War II. The new dogfight strategy was to hit and run, swooping down at full speed with a sudden blast of overwhelming firepower on opponents who never knew what hit them. That was the theory. In July 1944 at 30,000 feet over Austria, John would discover that any strategy that got you home alive was good dogfighting.

In September 1943, John was still learning the basics of fighter strategy. It was Michigan, not Austria, below as he played chase-and-kill with his new squadronmates. They were flying old P-40 Warhawks, long-nosed fighters with a large air intake hole just below the propeller. The hole suggested a mouth to ground crews, who liked to paint rows of shark teeth around the intake and a shark's eye on either side. The P-40 was America's top fighter plane before Pearl Harbor, but, nearly two years later, the Warhawk's design was aging badly. Both the Axis and the Allies had better aircraft, but the AAF had lots of P-40s—3,000 with another 1,000 on order. The AAF figured that

John is in the back row, fifth from the right, of Class SE 43-G at Tuskegee Army Airfield. John later added the black dots for classmates killed while flying, three in accidents and five in combat.

the Warhawks would be adequate for training and for use in lesser war zones with lesser units. The AAF expected that John's new squadron would be a lesser unit. It was one of the three additional Tuskegee fighter squadrons—the 100th, the 302nd, and John's 301st—that the AAF had rashly agreed to create following Pearl Harbor. The three new Tuskegee squadrons were supposed to form an all-black "fighter group," the 332nd Fighter Group. By late 1943, the AAF top brass had other plans for the Tuskegees—banishment.

John's future as a fighter pilot hung on the outcome of a *political* dogfight raging that fall in Washington, D.C. It was being fought at the highest levels between the AAF Command, the White House, Congress, and B. O. Davis, Jr., now Lieutenant Colonel Davis. Colonel Davis had just returned to the States from a forward combat airfield in Sicily, where he'd left the original Tuskegee squadron, the 99th, in combat. He'd been ordered home to take over the new Tuskegee fighter group that was forming in Michigan. When he got to Washington, Colonel Davis was jumped from behind.

The target was the 99th Squadron, but first they had to knock down Colonel Davis. He'd raised the 99th from scratch, transforming a paper unit with five pilots (counting himself) into a fully manned operational fighter squadron. When the colonel and his squadron finally arrived in North Africa in May 1943, the 99th was the only black squadron in the all-white Twelfth Air Force. The 99th was also the greenest. Stateside, white squadrons were always organized around a small core of combat veterans—staff officers who knew fighter operations, mechanics who knew field repairs, and a handful of veteran combat pilots who knew the tricks of their dangerous trade. The 99th arrived in North Africa with zero combat experience.

Officially, the 99th was one of three squadrons assigned to Colonel William Momyer's 33rd Fighter Group. In daily operations, Colonel Momyer and the two white squadrons in the 33rd Fighter Group shunned the 99th.

But Colonel Davis understood shunning. He set up the Tuskegee squadron on its own airstrip in the desert, took delivery of new P-40s, and began a do-it-yourself air war. The 99th would figure out for itself how to live in the mud, fix airplanes in sandstorms, and fly patrols without getting jumped.

The arrival of another fighter squadron, white or black, was of small interest to the top Allied commanders. They were concerned with grand strategy in the Mediterranean. Their objective was to cross from North Africa to the Italian mainland, knock Mussolini's fascist government out of the war, and drive the German armies back over the Alps. The Allied commanders planned to step across the narrow seas from North Africa to the Italian "boot" in a series of amphibious invasions, leaping from island to island to the mainland. Pantelleria was one of those steppingstone islands, but it was so tiny, it didn't seem worth a full-scale invasion. The Allied commanders gave the Twelfth Air Force the chance to "conquer" Pantelleria from the air alone. It was the first important combat assignment for the Tuskegee squadron. With Colonel Davis flying lead in his P-40, the 99th hammered the beach defenses at Pantelleria with dive bomb and low-level strafing attacks. Under furious bombardment from the whole Twelfth Air Force, the tiny island's tiny garrison surrendered.

In July, the Allied armies invaded the largest steppingstone island, Sicily. Flying cover for the Sicilian landings, a 99th pilot, Lt. Charles Hall, shot down a German FW-190. It was the squadron's first "kill," but it was a bittersweet victory. Two 99th pilots were killed the same day when their P-40s collided on takeoff. Air war eats rookies.

The conquest of Sicily gave the Tuskegees one small reward. They escaped Colonel Momyer. The 99th was transferred to the 79th Fighter Group in Sicily. Segregation was still AAF policy, but their new fighter group

The air assault on the little island of Pantelleria was the 99th Fighter Squadron's first big combat assignment. Back home, reports of their success sent the Negro press into jubilation.

commander was willing to work with Colonel Davis. Colonel Momyer, though, wasn't done with the Tuskegees. He carried his old grievances to Twelfth AF headquarters, harping on the 99th's "inadequate" performance under his command as clear proof that Negro pilots didn't belong in the AAF. Colonel Davis was all too familiar with that type of thinking but unaware of Momyer's private war. In early September 1943, Colonel Davis was promoted to full colonel and told to hand over command of the 99th in Sicily and come home to organize the new Tuskegee fighter group in Michigan.

The news must have unhinged Colonel Momyer. Within days, Momyer drew up a devastating report, citing the 99th's record for too many fatal accidents and too few enemy "kills." His deadliest fire was aimed at the Tuskegee pilots. They were cowards. Momyer wrote, "They failed to display the aggressiveness and daring for combat that are necessary to be a first class fighting organization."

Flying to war: The original Tuskegee fighter squadron, the 99th (badge at right), went into action on their own in 1943. John's 301st fighter squadron (badge at left) was part of the all-black 332nd fighter group. The 99th joined the group in 1944.

99th's movements
301st's movements
99th's debarkation
301st's debarkation
99th's victory sites
Allied landing sites

Jan 1944, 99th downs 12 enemy aircraft in dogfights over Anzio beachhead

SPIT FIRE

HUNGARY

PORTUGAL

YUGOSLAVIA

ITALY Ramitelli
May 1944

Anzio

Capodichino

Salerno

Taranto
Feb 1944

ATLANTIC OCEAN

MEDITERRANEAN SEA

Algiers

Tunis

Licata
July 1943

SPAIN

Casablanca
April 1943

ALGERIA

Isola di Pantelleria
99th's first victory

MOROCCO

TUNISIA

Momyer's boss, Col. Edwin House, warmly endorsed the memo, adding his personal opinion that "the Negro type has not the proper reflexes to make a first class fighter pilot." The Momyer memo climbed the chain of command all the way to Washington and the desk of General Henry H. "Hap" Arnold, commander of the U.S. Army Air Forces. For years, Hap Arnold had resisted Negro military aviation, and in Momyer's memo, General Arnold saw his last chance to squash it. General Arnold drafted his own memo for President Roosevelt's attention. "It is my considered opinion that our experience with this unit can only lead to the conclusion that the Negro is incapable of profitable employment as a fighter pilot in a forward combat zone," the general wrote. Arnold wanted President Roosevelt to downgrade the 99th and the other Tuskegee squadrons to permanent patrol duty. Segregated combat squadrons weren't an efficient use of war resources, Arnold concluded.

Ironically, the general was right, but for the wrong reasons. A segregated air force was hopelessly inefficient. Aircraft didn't have "white" and "colored" engines, yet the AAF had to have black and white mechanics. The AAF could swap engines but not mechanics between segregated squadrons. Segregating experience was even more wasteful. When the totally green 99th Squadron arrived in North Africa, it operated in a vacuum. Airplanes can't fly in a vacuum.

Down in Alabama, a white AAF officer was coming to the same shocking conclusion about segregation. Colonel Noel F. Parrish was the commanding officer of the Tuskegee program. The colonel was a native southerner, a former "pursuit" pilot, and a career army officer. Like most southern whites of his generation, Parrish arrived at Tuskegee believing that segregation was part of the natural social order. By the end of the war, Parrish had another word for it—*phony.* "There can be no consistent segregation policy because segregation is itself inconsistent and contradictory," Colonel Parrish wrote. "A segregated outfit always has a phony feel about it."

Back in Washington, there was nothing fake about the political attack on the Tuskegees. Momyer's "secret" memo had been leaked to *Time* magazine. By the time Colonel Davis reached Washington, newspapers were reporting that the 99th was already packing up for West Africa and never-ending patrol on its quiet Atlantic coast. Colonel Davis had been blindsided. He quickly called a Pentagon press conference and demanded a hearing before the War Department's committee on blacks in the armed forces. Davis knew that the 99th had mechanical troubles—too many accidents and breakdowns—but black aviation mechanics were nearly as hard to find in 1943 as black combat pilots. But it was Momyer's sneer about the Tuskegees' "lack of aggressiveness" that really rankled. Momyer had deliberately kept the 99th far away from likely combat areas until Pantelleria. But Colonel Davis took the blame on himself before the investigating committee. His leadership had been poor, he testified, because of his own lack of air combat experience.

If Colonel Davis was the public defender of black military aviation, the unsung hero of the day was Colonel Emmett O'Donnell, a white War Department staff officer who intercepted Arnold's proposal before it could reach the president's desk. O'Donnell recognized at once that Arnold's plan would set off a political firestorm among African Americans, already upset by the army's second-class treatment of black servicemen. O'Donnell wrote his own memo: "I feel that such a proposal to the president would definitely not be appreciated by him. He would probably interpret it as indicating a serious lack of understanding of the broad problems facing the country." O'Donnell's boss, General George C. Marshall, took his advice. The Arnold memo was quietly dropped.

The 99th, fighting in Italy, and the three Tuskegee fighter squadrons training in Michigan were saved. John and his squadronmates never realized how close they'd come to patrolling the Great Plains for submarines. At the time, John was more concerned about learning to fly a P-40. His "transition training" began back at Tuskegee when two beat-up P-40s were wheeled out for the use of twenty-seven would-be fighter pilots. One P-40 had a tendency to burst into flames during warm-up until the ground crews learned to start the engine with a fire hose at the ready. Once they'd moved to Michigan, the three squadrons of the 332nd Fighter Group were still short on working P-40s. John was frustrated. Every transition hour would be precious later in combat.

The P-39 Airacobra was America's oddest fighter plane. The cockpit doors swung open like car doors. The engine was behind the pilot's seat. The drive shaft and a 37-millimeter cannon that fired through the propeller ran between the pilot's legs. Worse, the P-39 was slow, a feeble climber, and useless at high altitudes. John's 332nd Fighter Group was the only AAF outfit in Europe flying P-39s.

In the end, the 332nd never flew the P-40 in combat. When Colonel Davis finally arrived in Michigan that October, he said nothing about the Great Washington Dogfight. He did announce that the new Tuskegee fighter group would be "transitioning" again to a new aircraft—the P-39 Airacobra. It was a one-of-a-kind name, and the Airacobra was unlike any other fighter in the American arsenal. It looked different. The P-39 had a "tricycle landing gear"; that is, it rested on a nose wheel and two wing wheels. The P-39 taxied with its nose and tail level to the runway, unlike "tail draggers" such as the P-40 (or the B-17), which rolled, nose up, on small tail wheels.

The P-39's landing gear was not its only peculiarity. To balance the aircraft, the engine was mounted *behind* the pilot. The drive shaft that turned the propeller (and fired a 37-millimeter cannon through the hub) ran between the pilot's legs. The very idea of that made pilots nervous. The cockpit doors were even more worrisome. Instead of sliding back or lifting up, the P-39's cockpit doors swung open on either side like car doors. John came to hate those doors. How could a pilot force open a side door to bail out if his P-39 went into a fatal spin stall? Worst of all, the P-39 was even slower than the P-40.

The P-39's inferior performance confirmed John's worst suspicions about the AAF. If Colonel Davis wouldn't talk about the Washington dogfight, his men could read reports in the Negro press. Then the Tuskegee rumor mill added its own theories. What Colonel Davis thought, no one knew. Colonel Davis did not discuss his thoughts or his orders with lower ranks. John would remember the colonel as a great leader but a distant and aloof figure. The colonel's orders, though, were always clear. Day after day, John stuffed himself into a P-39 cockpit and took to the air to build his hours and his mock dogfighting skills. Weeks passed. Flying hours accumulated. The AAF seemed in no hurry to rush the 332nd Fighter Group into war. Then, two weeks before Christmas 1943, the AAF changed its mind.

AAF typewriters went into furious action, "cutting orders" for the operations officer, the quartermaster, the flight surgeon, the provost marshal, and a long list of squadron adjutants. The 332nd Fighter Group was to leave its heavy equipment behind, including its P-39s. John's spirits rose. Maybe they'd never see the awkward Airacobras again. Everything else had to be packed up, typed up, and signed for. John gathered his personal gear ("Goggle Assembly, Flying, Type B-7, Cap, Flying Winter, Type B-2, Kit, Jungle Emergency, Type B-2 . . . Mattress, Pneumatic, Type A-3"), wrote home to say he was shipping out

A combat artist made this drawing of American soldiers wading ashore under enemy fire at Salerno during the long-anticipated Allied landing on the Italian mainland. The Tuskegee 99th Squadron followed along to provide air support and to prove themselves as fighter pilots.

but couldn't say where. On the day before Christmas, John boarded a train for Fort Patrick Henry in Virginia. There the men of the 332nd boarded a troop ship and waited to set sail for an undisclosed destination. The Tuskegee rumor mill pegged Italy. That's where the 99th Squadron was in action near Naples. On January 2, John lined up with the rest of the 332nd along the embarkation pier to wait his turn for a three-minute phone call home. On January 3, they were off. While the 332nd was still bouncing across the wintry Atlantic, the future of black aviation was decided at a place called Anzio.

Three months before, American and British forces had finally stormed ashore on the Italian mainland at Salerno, a small coastal city just above the ankle of the boot. The Allies quickly captured the ancient city of Naples and turned north, expecting to liberate Rome within weeks. A boot might be a handy metaphor for Italy's shape, but a long, narrow peninsula makes a perfect defensive position. The Germans dug in. The Allies bogged down. In November, the 99th Squadron moved with the rest of its fighter group from Sicily to airfields near Naples on the mainland so they could support the suffering Allied infantry.

In January 1944, the Allies launched a bold flanking attack, sending a large amphibious force to leapfrog north of and land behind the German lines at Anzio, a beach town just west of Rome. It was one leap too many. The Anzio beachhead was too far from friends and too close to the German reserves. The Germans counterattacked, bottling up the invaders on the beach and calling in the Luftwaffe to finish the job. The 99th was rushed into the air battle for Anzio. In two wild days—January 12 and 13, 1944—the Tuskegees shot down twelve enemy aircraft. The question of Negro aerial aggressiveness was settled.

The Anzio beachhead was saved, but the Germans adjusted their defenses and took a tighter grip on the boot. When John and the rest of the seasick 332nd Fighter Group finally stumbled ashore in February 1944, the crisis had settled back into stalemate. But the 332nd had arrived just in time for the Italian rainy season. John remembered his first journey through Italy as a nightmare of mud, rain, and military confusion. When his squadron finally reached their assigned airfield near Salerno, John's heart sank. Rows of new P-39Qs were waiting for them. The final insult came a few weeks later. A pair of Tuskegee P-39s on shipping patrol west of Naples spotted a German JU-88 bomber prowling at low altitude for a target. The Tuskegees swooped down, throttles wide open and guns blazing. The bomber gently accelerated and left the P-39s far behind.

Moving to the 15th Air Force on the east coast of Italy, the 332nd Fighter Group was re-equipped with P-47s with long-range fuel tanks to carry them on bomber escort missions.

If a P-39 couldn't chase down the enemy, a flight of them might drive off an intruder. John's squadron was assigned to "sit" air defense alerts. The routine went like this: A flight of four P-39s would park at the end of the runway, engines off and radios on, like taxis waiting for a fare. Strapped in, John could only prop open the P-39's carlike door with a stick and wait in the soft Italian springtime sun. It was a struggle not to doze off. Then—pop!—the tower shot off a flare. John was instantly awake. Coastal radar had spotted enemy bombers approaching Naples. The flight scrambled, heading out to sea as the tower radioed an intercept heading to the flight leader. Fortunately, most of the enemy intercepts were unescorted bombers who hurried out of range as the Tuskegees approached. But each time he scrambled in his slow, low-altitude P-39, John wondered what he would do if advanced German fighters were waiting for him. Weeks of sitting alerts and escorting ship convoys gave the Tuskegee rumor

The Republic P-47 "Thunderbolt."

mill time to debate whether they were
sitting ducks or permanent benchwarmers.
Either way, the rumor mill was certain that
the AAF command would stop at nothing
to shortchange the black man.

In May, the AAF command changed
its mind and changed their aircraft. The
332nd Fighter Group had been the only
American unit in Europe flying P-39s, and

it was getting embarrassing. Now their old P-39s were to be handed down
to Soviet allies on the Eastern Front. The 332nd would transition to P-47
Thunderbolts. Most fighter planes had long, thin noses because of their long,
thin "in-line" engines. The P-47 Thunderbolt had a barrel for a nose because
of its big, fat radial engine. Pilots called it the "Jug." By any name, the P-47
was huge for a single-seat fighter, but it was powerful, tough, and agile. It was
ideal for escorting medium bombers over the bogged-down Italian front.

A snapshot of Italy: The
Tuskegee squadrons scraped
out an air base from the
muddy fields around the
farming village of Ramitelli.
While high-altitude fighter
planes roared overhead, Italian
shepherds went about their
traditional routine.

The "Jugs" delivered to the 332nd were hand-me-downs, older C
models from white squadrons that were upgrading to brand-new D models.
Yet even secondhand P-47Cs were a vast improvement over brand-new P-
39Qs. John rejoiced in their power and speed. He also liked the new paint
scheme. The P-47s came in bare aluminum with a flat black antiglare strip
painted down the fat nose. To designate the 332nd Fighter Group, the tail
rudders of their P-47s were painted red. The nickname was inevitable—Red
Tails.

In June, the AAF command changed their mission again and the Red
Tails changed air forces, moving from the Twelfth Air Force based along on
Italy's western coast to the newly created Fifteenth Air Force setting up on
the eastern Adriatic side of the Italian boot. The mission of their old air force,

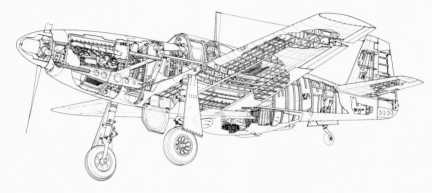

The P-51 Mustang was the best American fighter plane of World War II. The Tuskegees were originally equipped with older hand-me-down P-51s like this Model C, with its distinctive "greenhouse" canopy that aligns with the fuselage behind the pilot's head. As with all fighter planes, once you were strapped in for a five- or six-hour mission, your only place to go was through the rubber "pilot relief tube."

the Twelfth, had been "tactical," that is, to support the ground forces. The mission of the new Fifteenth was "strategic."

The Fifteenth was a bomber air force, waging its own strategic campaign directly against the Nazi empire. Its goal was the destruction of the "home front" industrial base that kept German armies in the field. Its punch was the long-range four-engine heavy bomber. The heavies—B-17s and B-24s—could hit targets hundreds of miles inside Austria, southern Germany, and the German-occupied countries to the east. To get there and back, the heavies needed long-range high-altitude fighter escorts. That was the 332nd's new mission. In June, the pilots ferried their P-47s across Italy to the Adriatic coast, where a new landing strip had been scraped out of the mud for them near the village of Ramitelli.

In July, the AAF command changed their aircraft *again*. Their new planes were P-51 "Mustangs," fitted with extra fuel tanks that extended their fighting range to 1,000 miles. This was John's fourth "transition" in two years to a new type of fighter aircraft. Once again, the P-51s delivered to the Red Tails were hand-me-downs, older Model B and Model C aircraft. The new P-51 Model D, with its distinctive wraparound "bubble" canopies, was going to white squadrons first. Still the P-51 was the best American fighter plane of the war, and John was delighted to have his hands on such a high-performance aircraft at last. Such a "hot" plane could be dangerous in the hands of inexperienced or out-of-practice pilots. A senior Tuskegee desk officer who hadn't kept up his flying hours was killed making a P-51 transition flight.

John remembered watching helplessly as an overconfident replacement pilot fresh from the States miscalculated a low-level loop and plowed his new P-51 into the ground.

To strengthen the Red Tails, the AAF command also sent the original Tuskegee squadron, the 99th, to join the 332nd Fighter Group at Ramitelli. The men of the 99th weren't happy about the transfer. Since Sicily, they'd been fighting alongside white squadrons and holding their own in P-40s against the Luftwaffe. Now the 99th was back in the old Jim Crow segregated Air Corps with a bunch of rookies. Whatever their grievances, Colonel Davis told his old squadron that he had new orders to go with their new red-tailed P-51s.

The colonel briefed each squadron himself. As John remembered it, Colonel Davis told them that the Fifteenth Air Force was having trouble with its fighter escorts. The pilots regarded bomber escort duty as beneath their dignity, the colonel said. These hotshots wanted to go after every Luftwaffe fighter in sight. Too many fighter escorts were peeling away from the Fifteenth Air Force bomber formations to chase after glory, leaving the heavies unprotected. This is not what the Red Tails were going to do, said Colonel Davis. "Your job is to escort these bombers, and I don't want to hear about any man leaving the bombers. You'll see enemy fighters out there, and everybody wants to be a hero. If the enemy comes in to attack, we'll take them on. If they stay out on the edge, we'll watch them, but we'll stay with the bombers."

John stayed with the bombers. The Tuskegees didn't score many air-to-air victories on escort missions, but the German interceptors soon learned to watch out for red paint. The red-tailed P-51s couldn't be lured away easily to chase a decoy attack. Flying escort, the Red Tails took their station well above the bomber stream, forcing German interceptors to make any attack below

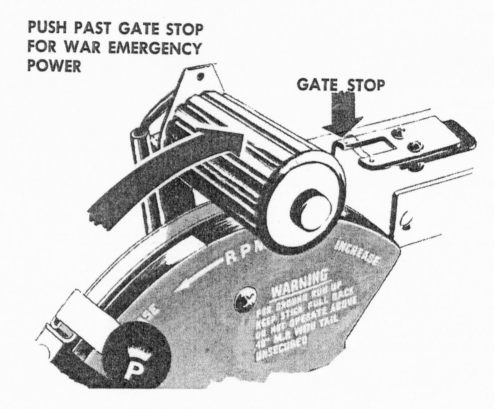

PUSH PAST GATE STOP FOR WAR EMERGENCY POWER

GATE STOP

R P M

INCREASE

WARNING
FOR GROUND RUN UP
KEEP STICK FULL BACK
OR DO NOT OPERATE ABOVE
45° M.P. WITH TAIL
UNSECURED

"The throttle reserve is called war emergency power," the P-51 pilot's manual warned, "and should be used only in extreme situations." The situation was beyond extreme, John decided over Linz, Austria. Guns frozen and trapped alone in a swarm of ME-109s, John slammed his throttle through the wire gate stop. The war emergency boost lifted his plane "like an elevator," John recalled, to safety.

them and in full view. That was the theory. In July 1944, John was in a flight of four P-51s flying above a bomber formation near Linz, Austria. Suddenly the sky around him was filled with German interceptors. "Break! Break! Break right!" screamed the flight leader. John followed him without thinking, breaking sharply right, but as he turned, John could see two Red Tails falling away behind them, on fire. And where was all this shooting coming from? To his horror, John realized that these German interceptors were attacking the escorts, not the bombers. Forty or more ME-109s had converged on a single flight of four Red Tails, determined to sweep them from the sky. John's was their flying bull's-eye.

He turned hard and hard again, and there for the first time in his AAF career was an enemy fighter plane moving directly into his gun sights. John pressed the trigger button. Nothing happened. John blinked in disbelief. His target disappeared. His flight leader was calling, "Leahr, where are you?" Lieutenant Leahr was turning for his life, forcing his P-51 into a tightening circle that brought him up behind the tail of another German. Again, he had one in his sights. Again, he pressed the trigger. Again, nothing happened. His machine guns were frozen solid. His armorer had reloaded them but forgot to plug in the heater that protected the guns at high altitude.

Without guns, escape was John's only strategy. He twisted his plane every which way, but at every turn, enemy planes and enemy cannon shells filled the sky. The hard turns were cutting his air speed now. Any second now, an interceptor would have John square in his gun sights. John made a quick promise to the Lord to live as a good Christian for the rest of his life (however long or short that might be), dropped his landing flaps, and slammed the throttle through the safety wire that fenced off the war emergency boost switch. The engine screamed a full note higher. John's P-51 went up like an elevator. When he leveled out, John was 1,500 feet above his nearest pursuer and heading for open sky.

It was the wildest dogfight of John's war. It was the only time he'd ever had an enemy aircraft in his sights, and yet he wasn't able to fire a shot. It was the closest he ever came to war's starkest commandment—kill or be killed. During his combat service, John fired off tens of thousands of rounds at ground targets, but whether he ever hit an enemy, John never knew and never wanted to know. Officially, he never scored a kill, confirmed or otherwise, of an enemy aircraft. But John came back from Linz in one piece, and that was victory enough for the day.

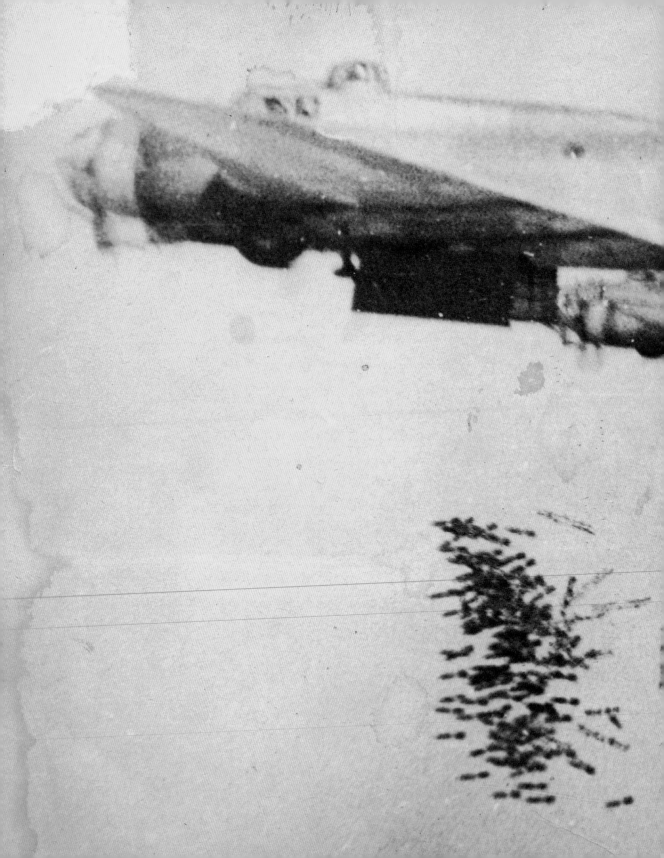

CHAPTER SIX
Bombers

Bombs away: On one of his final missions, Herb took this picture out the copilot's window just as his squadron released a blizzard of antipersonnel bombs on German infantry positions in northern Italy.

It was easy to make a fatal mistake and take nine other men with you. Herb learned that it didn't take a direct flak hit or a Luftwaffe interceptor belching cannon shells to knock you out of the sky. Flying in tight formation, Herb had only to hand off the controls to his copilot. Harry let the plane creep too close to the bombers ahead and stumbled into their prop wash, the highly disturbed air left by so many spinning propellers. In one sickening instant, the B-17 shook violently, stalled, and, flipping nearly upside down, fell like a brick through the squadron below them. "Herb, you take it," Harry screamed. We're dead, Herb thought, as he grabbed the controls back. He was nearly right. It was that easy.

A big plane like a B-17 could be surprisingly nimble. It could bank sharply, half roll, or pull up from a screaming dive. But a B-17 was not a fighter plane, and violently rolling a B-17 onto its back could snap off the wings. Somehow the wings stayed on as Herb's B-17 fell spinning through the formation. The B-17 was the last AAF heavy bomber without power assistance on the control cables. The force to move the rudder, ailerons, and elevators came directly from the arms and legs of the pilot and copilot. Now the copilot was frozen in shock. It was Herb alone pulling for life against the falling momentum of 60,000 pounds of aluminum, high-octane aviation fuel, bombs, and men.

Somehow Herb won out, yanking the plane through a half roll and flipping it right side up. Their plane had dropped clean through the formation and was now thousands of feet below and miles behind. Inside, everything that wasn't screwed down had come loose—maps, ammo, extra clothing, and crew members who hadn't been in their seats. But one by one everyone reported in over the intercom, shaken but okay. Everyone, that is, except the copilot. Harry was rigid in his seat, unable to speak and barely able to breathe. He was paralyzed by fear.

After the war, the AAF made a close study of fear. Former combat crew members were interviewed, and roughly 40 percent of them said they had been afraid on every or nearly every mission. Fifteen percent said they'd been so afraid at least once that they'd been unable to perform their duties; another 9 percent experienced this paralyzing fear more than once. Experience didn't help. The more missions the crew members flew, the more frightened they became. Well over half said their last mission was more terrifying than their first. The nature of their fears changed, too. On early missions, the fear was of failure or showing cowardice. On late missions, the fear was of being killed, wounded, or shot down and captured. As the fear piled up, a third of the crew members considered asking to be grounded. Four percent were. The polite term for the condition was "flak happy."

Fear had Herb's copilot by the throat. On his own, Herb wrestled the B-17 back into formation. Only then did Herb notice the pain in his shoulders. Pulling so hard and so suddenly, Herb had torn every muscle in his upper back. Now the pain spread down his legs and arms. No matter how much it hurt, Herb couldn't let go of the controls for a moment. His well-shaken B-17 was making strange noises. He sent the bombardier back to check the bomb load. Had something shifted? Had they broken the airplane's back in their wild fall?

His back and legs on fire, Herb flew the B-17 alone through the entire five-hour mission. Harry never said a word until they were nearly home. Surely Harry's career as a copilot was over. But at the debriefing critique, the group leader almost made a joke of it. "Who was that practicing inverted flying?" he asked. Harry raised his hand. Harry got off lightly from the colonel—a few days off the battle order to practice formation flying on his own. But Herb and Harry knew what had happened. Fear and mistrust sat between them in the cockpit after Harry finished his punishment. Meantime, the flight surgeon had examined Herb's back, prescribing whiskey for the pain and bed rest for the ache.

Herb's crew was not on the battle order the day after Christmas when Harry volunteered to fill an empty copilot's seat on another plane. This was common practice, a way for wounded or sick crew to catch up or even get ahead on their mission count. Herb was three missions ahead of his own crew because the group leader insisted that greenhorn pilots fresh from the States fly as copilots for their first taste of combat. No one thought there was anything remarkable about Harry volunteering as a substitute. Herb went into town. When he came back, a guard was sitting on Harry's bed, keeping watch on his locker. Harry's plane had been shot down.

Herb felt awful, although no one said much about Harry or the rest of the lost crew. That wasn't unusual. Ten days later, Harry came back. That was unusual. His shot-up B-17 had managed a crash landing in German-occupied Yugoslavia, where partisan fighters rescued the survivors. They were picked up by an AAF transport plane and, escorted by fighters, ferried back to Italy. Harry walked into the tent and asked where his stuff had gone. After that, Herb had his copilot back for good.

In the AAF, men came and went without warning. Herb's assignment to the 301st Bomb Group brought Lyle Pearson back into his life. In AAF terms, Herb and Lyle were old friends. Their friendship went back nearly a year. They'd been through B-17 pilot training together in New Mexico and then B-17 combat crew training in Texas. With orders to the same Overseas

That's Herb (first from right, first row) and Lyle Pearson (first from right, last row) graduating from bomber transition pilot training at Hobbs, New Mexico, in 1943. They would catch up a year later in Italy and then fifty years later by phone.

Movement center in Nebraska, Lyle and Herb figured that they had a good chance of assignment to the same outfit. Then Herb's waist gunner "missed movement." Herb went back to combat crew training to find a new crew. Lyle went off to war in a new B-17G.

When Herb finally landed in Italy in November 1944, he caught up with Lyle again in the 301st Bomb Group at Lucera. With his three-month head start, Lyle was no longer a greenhorn. Lyle's hat had the authentic "fifty mission crush" look, and his official mission count was not far behind. Lyle was nearly finished with his combat tour just as Herb's was beginning. Lyle also had the stories to go with the hat. He told Herb how he'd lost a B-17G to a duffel bag. As he was taking off from the Azores on his transatlantic ferry flight, a crewman's duffel bag stowed in the back of the plane had slipped free and jammed the tail plane elevator. Lyle's plane raced down the runway and, unable to gain an inch of altitude, ran straight into the harbor. His crew was unhurt. In a combat theater, no one cared about another crashed bomber. A week later, Lyle was flying in combat.

The operations officer of Herb's squadron works in the briefing room after the return from the day's mission. The crew names board is on the wall behind him.

Having Lyle around made Herb's transition to life on a combat airfield a little easier. They lived in a tent city. The bombers took off from runways surfaced with interlocking steel mats that had been laid directly over the Italian mud. To keep the mud out of their tents, the pilots dragged in surplus steel mats for flooring. Tent windows were made from Plexiglas salvaged from shot-up gun turrets. Tent stoves were empty gasoline drums fueled by high-octane aviation gasoline poured over bricks on the bottom and ignited by tossing in a match. Junked aircraft provided the raw materials for homemade chairs, dressers, and oil lamps. When it rained, everyone walked on wooden boardwalks

made from discarded packing crates. When it was windy, the airmen "borrowed" stone fences from the local farmers to reinforce tent walls.

The 301st was one of the first B-17 groups sent to Europe in August 1942. By the time Herb joined it in November 1944, the 301st Bomb Group had been in combat for thirty-seven straight months. Only a handful of senior officers and ground crew chiefs had been through the whole campaign. Crew members came and went, but the bomb group went on. By November 1944, each of the group's four squadrons had its operations "building" in a tent with plastered stone walls and a canvas roof. The order of battle was posted there every evening, listing the squadron crews flying the morning mission. Every morning, the crews were briefed there on the target for the day. Every afternoon, returning B-17 crews were debriefed there. The squadron operations officer and his staff questioned the crews about their actual routes to target, enemy fighters encountered, bombs dropped, damage observed, plus a hundred other details. The critique was typed up and rushed by jeep to Fifteenth Air Force HQ.

Every night, the operations officer prepared for the next day's mission. Cleaning up the squadron crew lists was the first step. Names were painted in white on black aluminum strips salvaged from crashed B-17s. The name strips were hung on nails in ten vertical columns. Each row down represented one of the ten crew slots on a B-17. Each row across was a complete crew. The aluminum name strips were easy to shuffle. Volunteers and replacements were slotted in to fill out rows. New crews were added across the bottom or slipped into empty rows. Empty rows were left by crewmen rotating home, missing, or dead.

Herb remembered his feeling of pride—and responsibility—the first time he saw "Heilbrun" on a nametag in the pilot's column, with the names of his crew filling out the row across. Then one evening, Herb walked through the briefing room just as the operations officer was finishing up the board. He had taken down the names of a missing crew and swapped in replacements, leaving the ten extra strips on his desk. The operations officer tossed them into the trash. Herb felt sick and then furious, but the officer was matter-of-fact. "Look, Heilbrun, I'm not happy about it either, but these guys aren't coming back here, or at least, not anytime soon. What else can I do with these things?"

"Hang on to mine," Herb told him: "I'll be back to get it. I'll be taking mine home."

If you're lucky, the operations officer probably thought but certainly didn't say.

CHAPTER SEVEN

The Target for Today

Bomber crews called it "sweating the string," and there really was a string. It was an ordinary piece of red string stretched from thumbtack to thumbtack across a large wall map of southern Europe. The string pointed the route that Herb's B-17 squadron would follow from its airfield in Italy to the bombing target for the day. On this day—December 16, 1944—the red string would remain a military secret until the mission briefing began at precisely "zero six hundred hours" (that is, 0600 by the army's twenty-four-hour clock, or six a.m. civilian time). The map rested, securely covered, on a stand at the front of the operations tent as the bomber crews strolled in from breakfast in the mess tent and noisily took their seats in the briefing room. They ignored the map. Everyone knew that today's string was already in place under the cover. In the small hours of the morning, a squadron operations officer had driven back from a briefing at Fifteenth Air Force headquarters, carrying aerial photographs, intelligence reports, and maps of the target. The operations staff then locked themselves away inside the operations tent and pressed thumbtacks marking the day's route into the big map. The string went on last.

A welcome sight: Tuskegee Red Tail escorts swoop down in their long-range P-51 Mustangs.

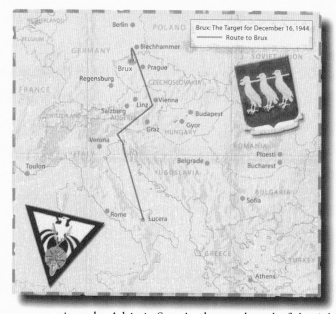

The first thumbtack was at Lucera, where Herb's B-17 bomb group was based. Lucera was on the back of the Italian boot, just above the heel. The toe side of the Italian boot pointed west into the Mediterranean Sea. The heel side pointed east into the Adriatic Sea. At the north end of the Adriatic was the mouth of the River Po and, just along the coast, the watery city of Venice. On December 16, 1944, the German army had the British and American ground forces pinned down south of the Po. Beyond the Po valley was the sharp, snow-covered high wall of the Alps. Beyond the eastern Alps was the enemy's industrial heartland. If the red string ran north across the Alps and into southern Germany, Austria, or the Nazi-occupied territories in Czechoslovakia, Poland, Romania, or Hungary, it was going to be a long mission for Herb's squadron.

Flying to Brux: Herb's 32nd Bomber Squadron (badge at left) was one of four squadrons in the 301st Bombardment Group (badge at right) on the mission.

At precisely 0600 hours, the operations officer stood up. The room went silent as his assistants uncovered the map. "The target for today is Brux," he said. The bomber crews read the string before he finished the sentence. It traced a long red line up the Adriatic and over the Alps toward a spot in German-occupied Czechoslovakia that the bomber crews knew well and dreaded. It was called "Brux" in 1944, the German name for a small industrial town where the Nazis had built a synthetic oil refinery. After the war, the Czechs would change the town's name back into their own language, turning "Brux" into "Most." It would be a small way to help rub out the horrors of the Brux oil refinery that the German occupiers built and rebuilt with slave labor and that the American bombers destroyed again and again.

Brux was just a name on a map for Herb on December 16, 1944. Back in November, when Herb and his crew were green replacements, they had been briefed for Brux. It would have been their first combat mission together as a crew. At that first briefing, the veteran pilots sitting near Herb groaned when they saw the red string to Brux. It would be nine hours in the air going and coming back, they told Herb—that is, if you made it back. At Brux, the Germans had hundreds of antiaircraft "flak" guns on railroad cars sheltering in mountain tunnels until the American bombers arrived. Then the flak cars came scooting out into daylight to blast away at the B-17s. The November mission to Brux had been washed out by weather, and Herb's squadron had been redirected to a secondary target at Salzburg, Austria. The Salzburg mission was eight hours long, but Herb and his crew came back unharmed. Now a month later, Brux was back on the map. Brux would be Herb's ninth mission. That left twenty-six to go.

His friend Lyle had told him to fly his missions one at a time. Today Herb tried to focus solely on Brux. Tomorrow was a long way off. The operations staff raced through the briefing: primary and secondary targets, the route going, the route coming back, rendezvous points, weather forecast, bomb load, radio codes, and the "recall" password, the secret code word that would abort the mission. The pilots, navigators, bombardiers, and radio operators had to note it all down, but even the crew gunners sat up to hear the latest intelligence on escape routes behind German lines. Everyone made note of the other important line on the big map. It showed the forward edge of the Red Army's advance into German territory. A bomber crippled deep inside Czechoslovakia might have its best chance of escape by turning east and crashing behind the Soviet front lines.

Flight crews were briefed with the latest on escape routes behind German lines. They were also given lightweight maps, survival rations, emergency medicine, and identity cards that asked for help in half a dozen languages. This was Herb's escape card. Fortunately, he never had to use it.

The B-17s would need two separate fighter escort groups for Brux. Fighters cruised at speeds one hundred or more miles per hour faster than the bombers. To stay close to the plodding bombers, fighter escorts had to burn off speed and fuel by making cutting S-turns and flying circles above the bomber stream. A single-seated fighter couldn't perform such tricks for nine hours without refueling, so the escorts would take Herb to Brux in relays. The first escort group would be flying P-38 Lightnings, rugged twin-engine fighters with twin-boomed tails. The P-38s would take the B-17s over the Alps into southern Germany. At that point, the P-38s would have just enough fuel to get home. Waiting for the handoff at 30,000 feet would be Herb's second escort, the 332nd Fighter Group in silver P-51s with red-painted tails. The Red Tails would take them the rest of the way to Brux. Stepping back when the B-17s started their bomb run, the Red Tails would wait for the bombers to emerge from the flak storm. Then the Red Tails would go to the aid of stragglers.

A few miles to the north at Ramitelli, John was getting his own briefing for Brux. On December 16, 1944, the 332nd Fighter Group would fly the second half of the escort. The speedy Red Tails would give the bomber force a two-hour head start and still catch up with them over target. The operations officer read out their orders: "You are to provide close escort on penetration, target cover, and withdrawal for B-17s of Fifth Bomb Wing to BRUX, Germany." The veteran Tuskegee pilots nodded silently at the name. The 332nd had flown escorts to Brux many times, but John realized that this would be his first mission there. How had he managed to miss Brux so far?

In six months of flying escort duty, John had been to all the other terrible targets, the nasty ones deep in enemy territory, ringed by antiaircraft batteries and haunted by Luftwaffe interceptors. John had flown missions to Linz, Vienna, Blechhammer, Gyor, and the worst of the worst, the Ploesti oil fields deep in German-occupied Romania. In the summer of 1944, the Fifteenth Air Force had launched its most daring long-range bombing raids of the war to choke off Hitler's last outside supply of oil. The strategic stakes were high at Ploesti. So were the American casualties. John flew to Ploesti five times. John would never forget the name or the sight of burning B-24s cartwheeling to earth with their crews trapped inside.

Brux would round out John's collection of terrible targets, a fitting end to his career as a Red Tail. Brux on December 16, 1944, was supposed to be John's last combat mission. By his own count, Brux would be mission number 132. According to AAF policy, that was impossible. A tour for fighters was supposed to be fifty combat missions. The squadron's official records said that Brux would be Lieutenant Leahr's seventy-second mission. That was malarkey. The Red Tails knew that their squadron clerks had unwritten orders to shave mission counts. Combat sorties were noted down as "practice" flights or never noted at all. A military historian who analyzed the Tuskegee squadron mission records after the war found that pilots in the 332nd often flew 125 sorties or more before completing an official 50-mission tour. It was the color line again. In 1942, the color line almost kept John out of combat flying. In 1944, it wouldn't let him go home.

The AAF didn't have enough black replacement pilots to rotate the original Tuskegees home. After the turmoil of creating four black fighter squadrons, the AAF throttled back on fighter pilot training at Tuskegee. The flow of new pilots was cut to a trickle. Once the four black fighter squadrons were in combat, there weren't enough replacements in the Tuskegee pipeline to cover losses, let alone to rotate the veterans home. If all the Red Tails at Ramitelli who'd flown fifty missions by December 16, 1944, had been allowed to go home, the 332nd Fighter Group would have shut down. By then, the Fifteenth AF couldn't spare the Red Tails. Of course, the Fifteenth

DATE	MAKE OF AIRCRAFT	CLASS	TYPE	CERTIFICATE NUMBER	MAKE OF ENGINE	H.P.	REMARKS OR INSPECTOR'S SIGNATURE CERTIFICATION NUMBER AND RATING
12-2-44	BOEING	B-17	G	U.S. ARMY	WRIGHT	4800	MISSION # 8
12-3-44	BOEING	B-17	G	U.S. ARMY	WRIGHT	4800	PRACTICE MISSIO
12-6-44	BOEING	B-17	G	U.S. ARMY	WRIGHT	4800	30 MIN. A.I. RETURN DUE TO WEATH
12-10-44	BOEING	B-17	G	U.S. ARMY	WRIGHT	4800	2:30 "A.I." "
12-11-44	BOEING	B-17	G	U.S. ARMY	WRIGHT	4800	PRACTICE GUNNERY
12-16-44	BOEING	B-17	G	U.S. ARMY	WRIGHT	4800	MISSION # 9
12-17-44	BOEING	B-17	G	U.S. ARMY	WRIGHT	4800	MISSION # 10
12-18-44	BOEING	B-17	G	U.S. ARMY	WRIGHT	4800	MISSION # 11
12-20-44	BOEING	B-17	G	U.S. ARMY	WRIGHT	4800	MISSION # 12
12-25-44	BOEING	B-17	G	U.S. ARMY	WRIGHT	4800	MISSION # 13
12-27-44	BOEING	B-17	G	U.S. ARMY	WRIGHT	4800	MISSION # 14

I HEREBY CERTIFY THAT THE FOREGOING ENTRIES ARE TRUE AND CORRECT.

SIGNED *Herbert M. Heilbrun*

AF couldn't allow white replacement pilots to fly in black squadrons, so creative record-keeping was the only answer. John had been in combat for ten straight months by December 1944 before he became the first pilot in his squadron to be offered a rotation home. Officially, he would complete his 50-mission tour, even if Brux would be John's mission number 132. Of course, John first had to survive Brux.

That was the little picture for Herb and John on December 16, 1944. In the big picture, the Fifteenth Air Force was sending two "bomber wings" to hit Brux, one after another, with only ten minutes between attacks. Each wing would send six "bomb groups," and each group would send twenty-eight planes for a combined strike force of 336 bombers. Thirty-four P-38s would fly the first escort leg with fifty red-tailed P-51s waiting to meet the bombers near the target. All these wings, waves, and escorts had to come together over Brux in a precise order and on a tight timetable.

Herb's bomber group, the 301st, was in the first strike wave. The B-17s began takeoff from Lucera at 0815 hours, heading out over the sea for the elaborate aerial square dance that would transform twenty-eight airplanes into two compact "elements." The trick was not to get too close to the echelon

| CROSS COUNTRY | | TIME | | | | | |
FROM	TO	INSTRUMENT RADIO OR HOOD	DUAL AS INSTRUCTOR	DUAL AS STUDENT	SOLO DAY	SOLO NIGHT	DAILY TOTAL TIME
BLECHAMMER, GERMANY	TARGET				8 50		8 50
	LOCAL				4 10		4 10
SPLIT, YUGOSLAVIA					4 30		4 30
44° 07'N					3 20		3 20
	LOCAL				2 05		2 05
RUX, CZECHOSLAVAKIA					9 10		9 10
ECHHAMMER, GERMANY					9 00		9 00
ECHHAMMER, GERMANY					9 00		9 00
GENSBERG, GERMANY					8 10		8 10
UX, CZECHOSLAVAKIA					9 05		9 05
NZ, AUSTRIA					8 15		8 15
TOTAL					75 35	−	75 35
AMT. FORWARD					60 00	4 10	64 10
TOTAL TO DATE					135 35	4 10	139 45

forming in front of you and slam into their prop wash. The B-17s took off in squadrons of seven planes and quickly formed into a group of twenty-eight. Stacked in three layers and bristling with defensive machine guns, the B-17s formed a virtual flying fortress. Herb's bomb group headed for the rendezvous with two others over a large coastal lagoon. It was an easy landmark, and the groups all arrived on time. They reshuffled their sections into two attack waves and headed north up the Adriatic.

But the mission plan was already fraying. At the last minute, Fifteenth Air Force Headquarters had scrubbed two bomb groups—fifty-six aircraft— from the attack without telling the third group. Fourteen of those planes arrived at the correct rendezvous point but found it empty. They attacked Brux on their own. The other fourteen reached the wrong rendezvous point and found no one there. They attacked a secondary target. All this left the main force heading for Brux eighty-four planes short.

Herb knew nothing about this high-level confusion. He was focused on his squadron leader, flying above and to his right. Herb's job was to hold position and follow the squadron leader's every move. He didn't notice the first escort group of P-38s take station above the bombers until his tail gunner

Herb's flight logbook for December 1944. Brux was "Mission #9" on December 16. Herb was in the air for nine hours and ten minutes.

called out the sighting over the intercom. Crossing the Alps, Herb caught glimpses of the mountains below through breaks in the high cirrus clouds. North of the Alps, the clouds thickened and the ground was completely hidden. The formation had been steadily climbing in the three hours since takeoff. They squeezed over the Alps at 27,000 feet and pressed north toward southern Germay and the IP—the Initial Point—where the bomb run would begin.

The Red Tails were waiting at 30,000 feet. The P-38s peeled away, their mission completed. So far, it had been a long but uneventful flight. Herb's gunners had spotted three ME-109s on the Italian side of the Alps, but the German planes fled at the sight of so many bombers and escorts. German interceptors were far fewer now and reluctant to tackle big formations. They preferred to pick off stragglers and cripples. The Red Tails were there to discourage them. But once the Red Tails brought them to the IP, the bombers were on their own for the most dangerous part of the mission—the flak storm. At the IP, the bombers locked themselves into a rigid band, three layers deep, flying in one direction at one speed. This was how the bombardiers took aim.

The Americans bombed by geometry. In clear weather, they bombed by geometry and optics. The optical bombsight was a sophisticated mechanical "computer" that employed gears, lenses, and gyroscopes instead of modern computer chips to compute the precise moment for "Bombs away." But on December 16, 1944, the thick cumulus cloud layer over Brux made the optical bombsight useless. For cloudy weather, they bombed by geometry and radar. Special Pathfinder aircraft equipped with the latest "PFF" radar bombsight led the Brux attack. In 1944, radar bombsights were primitive and especially vulnerable to vibration. A B-17 bouncing along at 27,000 feet with shells exploding all around vibrated like crazy. If the vibration broke a vacuum tube, the Pathfinder's radar bombsight would cut out, leaving the bombers blind. Whether guided by radar or optical sights, the bomber stream had to come in straight and level from the IP. That made the B-17s perfect targets for antiaircraft gunners.

The Germans shot down bombers by geometry. On clear days, the antiaircraft gunners used optical range finders, giant binoculars that gauged distance by measuring the angle between lenses. The range finder operator dialed the angle into a drumlike mechanical calculator, which computed the settings for gun elevation, direction, and fuse delay. A speeding cannon shell takes several seconds to reach 27,000 feet. Instead of aiming directly at a flying bomber, the antiaircraft cannon aimed at the point where the range calculator said the B-17 would be several seconds later when the shell exploded.

On cloudy days, the antiaircraft gunners used radar range finders. Fortunately for Herb, German radar range finders were also primitive and unreliable in 1944. So were the gun crews themselves. Most of the gunners were bottom of the barrel—underage teenagers, invalids, and old men. With such crews, their flak battery commanders used cruder aiming methods. They knew exactly where the American bombers were going at Brux—the synthetic oil refinery. They preset their guns and fuses to project a "box barrage," a rectangle in the sky, directly above the oil refinery. The teenage gunners had only to fire into the box. To bomb the refinery, the bombers had to fly straight through it.

At the IP, Herb's flight engineer came forward to dress him for the flak. The crew was already suited up for the attack, but Herb and his copilot were too busy at the controls to spare a hand for themselves. Like a medieval squire dressing a knight for battle, the flight engineer draped a heavy flak jacket of canvas and steel plates over Herb's shoulders and lap. The temperature outside the B-17 was forty below. Herb was already wearing long wool underwear, his regulation wool uniform, and a heavy, full-length canvas flight suit. At 27,000 feet, everyone on board was breathing oxygen through rubber masks. The engineer pulled antiflash goggles down over Herb's eyes and crushed a modified infantryman's steel helmet onto his head. Dressed like this, Herb might survive a near miss that sprayed the cockpit with red-hot shrapnel and flying glass. Nothing would protect him against a direct hit. The engineer turned and dressed the copilot.

Outside Herb's cockpit, it was eerily peaceful. The ground was completely hidden. Only distant mountains showed through the heavy cumulus clouds. High above, the silver bombers dashed along in fierce sunshine. The box barrage appeared dead ahead. That was Brux.

John had the better view. As the bomber stream flowed toward Brux, the Red Tails climbed above them to 30,000 feet and took station to one side. They were bystanders. The battle now was between the heavy bombers and the flak gunners. The box barrage over Brux swelled into a black thundercloud, lit from within by exploding shells. John scanned the blue-domed sky for Luftwaffe "bandits." Overhead, he could see only the vapor trails of other Red Tail escorts circling above the battle. Below, the bombers plowed on toward the flak cloud.

John had seen this awful sight before. Over Blechhammer, over Vienna, over Linz, but most of all over Ploesti, John had seen the bombers disappear into the box barrage. While he waited so high above, no sound reached him. John could only count the flashes. At Ploesti, the B-24s went in at a lower altitude to be sure of their target. The B-24s caught special hell. John saw them fall, wings gone, cockpit gone, or tail gone. Sometimes, a string of parachutes opened behind a falling plane. Sometimes there were none. At Ploesti, John saw a B-24 vanish in one bright flash, a direct hit in the bomb bay. Luftwaffe fighters were prowling in force at Ploesti, and the Red Tails swooped down as the B-24s came staggering out of the flak cloud, herding the crippled bombers away before the German interceptors could strike.

At Ploesti, a straggler was in deep trouble a long way from home. Maybe the B-24 came out of the flak with a couple of engines knocked out. Maybe the plane was burning. The Red Tails closed in. Sometimes a pilot got his plane together and crept away on two engines, a pair of Red Tails following. Sometimes the Red Tails could only witness where the straggler went down, and whether there was smoke or chutes. The bombers always called the escorts "Little Friend," and coming away from Ploesti, John remembered the bomber-to-escort radio channel filled with voices calling, "Little Friend, Little Friend, I'm going down" or "Little Friend, I'm losing altitude. Can you see us? Is our tail gunner dead?" or "Little Friend, our pilot's dead. The copilot's injured. Stay with us, Little Friend. Stay with us."

The Red Tails stayed with the stragglers until their fuel gauges forced them to run for home. It wasn't glamorous work. Hotshot fighter pilots and hotshot squadrons hated bomber escort duty, but Colonel Davis wasn't taking any excuses. John stayed with the bombers.

At Brux on December 16, 1944, Herb had never seen anything like the flak storm exploding just outside his window. And yet he was too busy to be scared. Instead, Herb got off a brief prayer and went back to the vital business of holding his place in formation. Then the Pathfinder signaled "Bombs away" and Herb's bombardier released their twelve 500-pound bombs. Herb felt the plane leap as the bomb load tumbled away. Then Herb was past the target and he climbed hard toward the waiting Red Tail escorts. The formation turned east toward Prague and then southwest toward the Alps. Herb craned his neck to survey his squadron. Everyone was still there. Everyone was still flying. One B-17 in his group was damaged but made it home anyway. No one in Herb's B-17 group was killed or seriously wounded at Brux. The B-24s in the next wave were not as lucky. The Red Tail leader had to send two planes back to search for a damaged B-24 calling for a Little Friend.

The raid on Brux was not a turning point in the war. Bloodier events were afoot on December 16, 1944, for the Battle of the Bulge started that day. On the French-Belgian border, Hitler staked his final bet, throwing in his reserves—200,000 soldiers and his last armored Panzer divisions—on a gamble. Hitler would stop the American army with a surprise attack through the "impenetrable" Ardennes forest. Early that morning, Hitler's Panzers smashed through the woods and cut off a huge pocket of American defenders—the Bulge, the GIs inside called it—around the Belgian city of Bastogne.

Compared to the Battle of the Bulge, the air battle that day over Brux was a sideshow. But December 16, 1944, was important for John and Herb. It was their last mission together, even if neither of them knew it. Herb and John had actually flown together once before in early December against the synthetic oil refinery at Blechhammer. They never knew that, either. A world war covers a lot of ground, and the chances of two guys from the same Cincinnati elementary school meeting up in Italy were not great. John's brother, Bill, who started out in a segregated cavalry regiment, had ended up stationed near Naples with his segregated engineering battalion. Soldiers weren't allowed to write home and tell their families where they were serving, but somehow John got word that Bill's unit was in Italy. John commandeered a jeep for the day and dropped in on his flabbergasted brother.

But imagine John and Herb eating at the same hotel or drinking in an officers' club in Naples. They exchange flying stories. They discover that they're both from Cincinnati.

Finding Bill: Servicemen overseas weren't allowed to write home and tell their families exactly where they were serving and what they were doing. You could, however, give broad hints. Or you could also ask around on the army grapevine, which is what John did to track down his brother Bill's field engineering battalion serving in Italy.

They discover that they both had Miss Pitchell in the third grade. That was impossible in 1944. Because of the color line, Lieutenant Heilbrun had a better chance of meeting the supreme allied commander, General Eisenhower, in Italy than of meeting Lieutenant Leahr.

December 16, 1944, was a critical day for Herb. His plane came through the flak storm at Brux, but the violence shook him. Herb wondered if he could make it through twenty-six more missions like Brux. He was at the wheel of his B-17 for nine hours and ten minutes. Back at Lucera, he no sooner fell asleep than his navigator shook him awake. They were on the battle order again for tomorrow, the navigator told him. Breakfast at 0500 hours. Briefing at 0600 hours.

For John, the combat war ended on December 16, 1944. When the Red Tails touched down, all safe, at Ramitelli that afternoon, John had been in the cockpit for five hours and forty minutes. Added to all his other numbers—sorties, missions, types of aircraft flown, months in combat—it was finally John's time to go home. John shook hands all around the squadron, packed his gear for shipment home, and hopped a ferry flight to Naples. There John was stranded by the Battle of the Bulge. Everything that floated or flew was heading east with reinforcements for the besieged defenders of Bastogne. It was four weeks before John could find an officer's berth on a troop ship heading west toward home. Once on board, John was startled to discover that his three cabinmates were white. It was John's first integrated assignment in the U.S. Army. Unfortunately, it was his last. A different war awaited John stateside.

End of the 35th mission,
April 16 - 1945.
— 1st Lt. Herbert M. Heilbrun. —

CHAPTER EIGHT

V for Victory

After Brux on December 16, Herb's crew was on the battle order for Blechhammer on December 17. Blechhammer was another top-priority target, a synthetic oil refinery in what is now southern Poland. It was heavily defended by flak and a long way from home. This time, the Luftwaffe came out in force to stop Herb's bomber group. For weeks, the bomber crews had seen only small flights of German interceptors chasing after stragglers or scurrying away at the first sight of the Little Friends. On December 17, the Luftwaffe sent eighty or ninety FW-190s straight at them. The Little Friends escorts held them off in a running dogfight, but the bombers were only dimly aware of what was going on above them. The flak coming up at them from Blechhammer was ferocious. Over target, a B-17 in Herb's group was hit square in the number three engine. The formation watched as the crippled plane turned east, trying for the safety of the Soviet front lines. It didn't make it, crashing inside Nazi-held Poland. Herb logged nine hours at the controls flying to Blechhammer and back. Herb remembered his flight engineer coming to him that night to tell him that they were on the battle order the

Home safe: Herb leans against the propeller of "Haley's Comet" after his 35th and last mission, April 16, 1945.

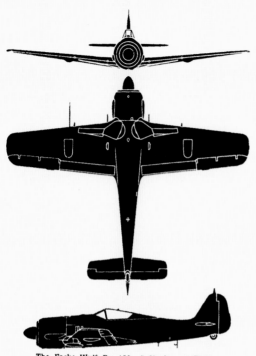
The Focke-Wulf Fw 190A-5 Single-seat Fighter.

Spotting enemy aircraft: Silhouettes were used to teach aircraft recognition. These are two of Germany's best interceptors. The Messerschmitt 109 (right) was a deadly new type of fighter when Hitler first unleashed it during the Spanish Civil War in 1936. The ME-109 was continually updated and improved throughout the war but the basic design was showing its age by 1945. In the air war's final months, the Focke-Wulf 190 (above) was being drastically modified as a super-high-altitude interceptor that could disrupt the high-flying B-17.

next day, the third day in a row. "They can't do this to us," said the flight engineer.

"Here's my theory," Herb told him. "We're going to fly whatever airplane they give us. We're going to fly it to wherever they tell us."

It was Brux again. This time, German fighters got past the Little Friends and tore through the bomber stream, firing wildly. The Flying Fortress gunners met them with a storm of .50 caliber bullets. Amazingly, neither side scored a kill, but over target, the flak gunners brought down a B-17 in Herb's group. Herb came through untouched. Brux was nine hours there and back, bringing his total to just over twenty-seven hours of combat flying in three days. He staggered to his tent and fell instantly asleep, still wearing his flight suit, pistol holster, and fur-lined boots. In the night, someone took off his boots and covered him up. They let him sleep, because Herb was off the next morning's battle order.

On Christmas Day, 1944, Herb's bomb group went back to Brux. "It was not one of the better days for the 301st," said the official history. It was one of the worst days of Herb's life. Half the bomber force never made it to Brux because of the weather. Herb was in the half that did. The weather was so thick and the radar so bad that the Pathfinder had to make three passes at the target before ordering "Bombs away." That gave the flak barrage three chances at them. "The only bright note was that no airplane was lost," the official history noted, "although flak caused major damage to one plane."

That was Herb's plane. Shells exploding just outside the aircraft peppered the interior with white-hot shrapnel. The tail windows were shot out and a waist gunner was hit in the foot. Shrapnel struck the plane so many times that Herb saw clouds of dust rising from the floorboards. His B-17 was being beaten like a carpet on a clothesline. On the run to target, Herb reached down to adjust a switch on the cockpit wall, located a few inches from his knee. His hand found only empty air. There was a neatly punched hole where the switch had been. Through the hole, Herb could see the sky filling with filthy puffs of smoke from exploding flak shells. And yet Herb's B-17 kept flying. Back at base, his crew chief counted eighty-nine flak holes in the plane and presented Herb with a shrapnel souvenir. The flak metal was blackened but cool to the touch now. Herb hefted it in his hand, wondering how something so destructive could come so close and yet not harm him.

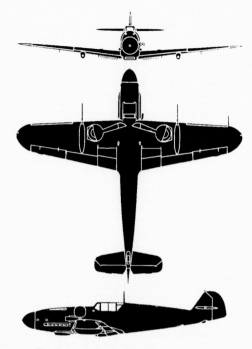

The Messerschmitt Me 190ᴳ Single-seat Fighter.

The winter grew darker for Herb. It was against regulations, but he kept a personal diary of his combat tour. The AAF worried that a combat diary could fall into enemy hands and reveal military secrets, but Herb's secrets were personal. His first entries were anxious but upbeat. Herb also pasted in copies of prayers that he could recite under his breath during a bomb run. Putting his fate into the hands of the Almighty let Herb concentrate on flying his B-17. But how long would he beat the odds and dodge the shrapnel? Would his aluminum name strip end up in the trash can?

Lyle's example gave him hope. Nearing the end of his tour, Lyle calculated that he could celebrate New Year's 1945 with orders for home in his pocket. On December 29, Herb and Lyle were both on the battle order for the railroad yards at Innsbruck, Austria. It would be mission number fifteen for Herb, not even halfway home. For Lyle, it would be the end of his tour. At the operations briefing, Herb turned around in his seat and told Lyle that they should go into town afterward and really hang one on in celebration. Lyle's second child had been born while he was in Italy, and Herb knew Lyle was looking forward to finally getting to hold the new baby. Out on the flight line, Lyle's ground crew rolled out a brand-new B-17G, freshly delivered from the States, for his last mission.

Over the Alps, the formation was knocked about by extremely strong winds. The weather on the Austrian side was worse. The Pathfinder aborted their primary target at Innsbruck and turned the formation around. They headed back over the Alps at the Brenner Pass to hit a secondary target, a locomotive repair shop, on the Italian side. Crossing back over the Brenner Pass, Lyle's plane was hit twice by German flak guns, once in the bottom turret and once in the still-loaded bomb bay.

That evening, Herb's diary was down to bare facts. "Lyle was shot down today. I saw most of it, as he was flying in the lead, right in front of us. He must have gotten a direct hit. The ship peeled out of formation in a gentle bank in front of us. Both pilots must have been hit because they never came out of it. My right waist gunner picked them up (visually) and told me on the interphone what happened. Both wings came off. They hit the mountain and blew up. It was all over in thirty seconds and no chutes came out."

The New Year opened gloomily for the Allies. Counterattacks had rescued the defenders of the Bulge and driven the Germans back, but Allied

One of Herb's waist gunners reported seeing Lyle Pearson's B-17 explode in flames over the Alps in December 1944. Fifty years later, Herb got a different view of the crash. Illustration from USAAF B-17 pilot's manual.

hopes of quick victory in Europe were shattered. The Nazis were not finished yet. Then the Japanese would have to be defeated with bloody, island-by-island steppingstone landings across the Pacific. There would be plenty of time to get killed in 1945.

The weather matched Herb's mood. Heavy winds, dense clouds, and winter storms halted operations for days. In January 1945, the whole 301st Bomb Group flew only seven missions. Herb went on two of them, both times to the Vienna railroad freight yards where the crews were briefed to expect "heavy and intense flak." The flak claimed one B-17 over Vienna, but Herb's group came through with only minor damage. Still, Herb wondered when he would fly into another deathtrap like Brux or the Brenner Pass.

On February 1, 1945, Herb found himself in a deathtrap, only it was his own side that nearly killed him. It was mechanical failure, not flak. The mission was an oil refinery at Moosbierbaum, just outside Vienna. The weather was still awful. The B-24s, which flew at lower altitudes, were more vulnerable to bad weather, so the pressure was on to get as many high-altitude B-17s as possible into the attack force. That put the major in charge of the repair shops for Herb's squadron under the gun. The night before Moosbierbaum, Herb's crew was on the order of battle, but rumor said that there weren't enough airworthy B-17s for such a big mission. The major promised a maximum repair effort overnight. Herb had no idea what he would be flying in the morning.

Crews always had favorite aircraft, but except for the special Pathfinder ships, no crew had a guarantee of getting their "own" plane. When the squadron's original crews landed in England in 1942, every B-17 commander had a "personal" aircraft, usually with a sweetheart's name or a racy pinup picture or a slogan painted on the nose. As those planes were damaged or their crews went home, they passed into a general pool to be patched up or refitted for newcomers. Replacement crews quickly learned which B-17s were the trusty ones and which the dangerous "crates." The more missions you flew, the more likely you were to get a plane you trusted or even a brand-new B-17G. Herb's crew preferred "Haley's Comet," a bright metal B-17G named by a previous crew after Jack Haley, the actor who played the Tin Man in the *Wizard of Oz* movie. Maybe the bare aluminum reminded the namers of the Tin Man. If Haley's Comet was on the flight line, Herb's crew wanted to fly it.

The Comet was out of action for Moosbierbaum; they would have to take the luck of the draw. But when Herb reached his assigned aircraft on the flight line, he was stunned. It was a crate, an orphan B-17 from the Eighth Air Force in England that had crash-landed behind Soviet lines, been patched together, and flown out to Italy. It belonged to no one now unless the major's repair crews tore it apart for spares or converted it into a squadron "hack," a stripped-out bomber good enough to fly men to Naples or Rome on leave. Suddenly this old crate was pretending to be a bomber again, sitting there fueled, armed, and bombed up to join the order of battle. When Herb reached the cockpit and pulled out the plane's logbook, he felt sick. The engines had 521 hours on them. Herb knew from his time at Wright Aero that an aircraft engine with close to 500 hours on it wasn't safe. After 500 hours, an engine needed a total teardown and rebuild. To fly this crate on a combat mission was crazy. But it was too late. Planes all around them were going through the engine start drill. Any minute, the colonel's ship would be rolling toward takeoff. The rest of the squadron had better be with him at 10,000 feet and building the attack formation within minutes. Herb remembered what he'd told his flight engineer before Brux: "We're going to fly whatever airplane they give us. We're going to fly it to wherever they tell us."

Herb glanced across at Harry in the copilot's seat. There was nothing to do but start the engines and pray. Maybe an oil seal would blow on Engine Start. None did. Herb took off, climbed to his assigned position in the formation, and set out for Moosbierbaum. All four engines were running, but Herb was worried. To keep up with the formation, he couldn't nurse his suspect engines. As the bombers crossed the Alps into southern Austria, the number one engine began to smoke and then vibrate violently. Herb shut it down and managed to "feather" the dead propeller; that is, he rotated the blades into a neutral position to minimize air resistance. Unfeathered, a frozen prop would drag them down as surely as if the airplane had a ship's anchor dangling from the wing.

Now it was equally dangerous to turn back alone or go on with the formation to target. Running on three engines, Herb ordered the bombardier to jettison half the bomb load. The barrage tore up the Austrian pastures below them, but the lighter airplane picked up a little speed. They would be able to stay with the formation, Herb thought, if nothing else went wrong. Then engine number three erupted in smoke and violent vibration. Herb feathered the prop. On two engines, they were finished, at least, with this mission. Herb lowered and raised the plane's wheels, the signal to his squadron leader that he was aborting, and turned his crippled crate south toward home.

Moosbierbaum was waiting for the rest of Herb's bomb group with bad flak and terrible weather. The flak claimed two B-17s, and the weather scattered the attackers. But Herb and his crew were already fighting for their lives. The enemy was gravity. To get home, they had the Alps to scale first, and Herb would need every inch of altitude the plane could grab to get over on two engines. He ordered the rest of the bomb load jettisoned. The B-17 gained a little height, but the snowy mountaintops ahead still looked much too close for comfort. They had no Little Friends to protect them, but they had no choice. The guns had to go. Herb ordered·the gunners to heave their heavy .50-caliber machine guns overboard, followed by anything else the crew could tear loose—the oxygen cylinders, ammunition, extra clothing, flak jackets, and helmets. They kept the radio, their parachutes, and the navigation chart. Somehow, they scraped over the Alps without attracting Luftwaffe attention. Herb recited one of his silent prayers, asking only to reach the coast. The minutes ticked by. Herb caught a glint of sunlight ahead, flashing off the Adriatic. Then Herb saw a thin stream of oil drizzling out of engine number two. A B-17 can't fly on one engine, at least not for long.

Herb prayed, "Dear Lord, please just get me halfway down the Adriatic." His radioman made contact with an American flight control station so at least someone would now know where they went down or if they bailed out. Herb, though, was determined to go home. He radioed ahead to the airfield, asking for fire engines and ambulances on the runway. Number two was leaking heavily now. Herb figured that he had one pass at a landing. They were too low to bail out now, and too crippled to go around the field again. It was land or crash. On February 1, 1944, Herb made the best landing of his life in the worst airplane he ever flew. He let the crate roll all the way down to the end of the runway before coming to a stop. The crew climbed out, giddy with relief. They were home, safe, sound, and dry.

The major came roaring up in a jeep. A magnificent landing, the major shouted, a magnificent achievement to make it back on two engines. "Lieutenant Heilbrun, you'll probably get the DFC for this," said the major, meaning that Herb would get the Distinguished Flying Cross, one of the AAF's highest honors. What Herb almost got was a court-martial. For the next five minutes, the lieutenant told the major precisely what the lieutenant thought of someone who would send ten men on a bombing mission in an aircraft with more than five hundred hours on the engines. "Criminal" was one of the more polite words Herb used. Lieutenants did not talk this way to majors in the AAF, especially with so many enlisted men and officers standing around, soaking up every word. And yet Lieutenant Heilbrun said all that and walked away from the major. Maybe that was another reason for the DFC that Herb was awarded for actions above and beyond the call of duty on February 1, 1945.

After that, Herb gave up his diary entirely. Gradually, the missions became a little easier. Herb still flew deep into Germany and Austria, but now the war was clearly turning in the Allies' favor. The Red Army was steadily advancing on the German capital of Berlin from the east. One morning in the operations tent, the line on the map that showed the Soviet front was moved past Vienna. The crews cheered. They would never face "heavy and intense flak" over Vienna again. The Luftwaffe was running low on pilots but not on aircraft. The latest German interceptor, the ME-262, was the world's first operational jet fighter. The Allies had nothing like it. The Luftwaffe jet could climb higher, dive harder, and shoot harder than any Little Friend escort. But the Luftwaffe was running low on fuel for jets and for training jet pilots, thanks to the relentless bombing raids on oil refineries.

The Red Tails who continued to fly bomber escort missions from Ramitelli in 1945 soon got the measure of the new German jets. On March 24, 1945, the Red Tails shot down three ME-262s during a raid on Berlin. Combat veterans in propeller-driven P-51s won out over Luftwaffe rookies in jets. By then, a Red Tail escort had become a beautiful sight for Fifteenth Air Force bomber crews.

By April 1945, Herb's squadron was flying "close support" missions to help the weary Allied infantry grinding its way north up the Italian peninsula. The Germans still had flak guns, but Herb figured that if his ship was hit, he could glide back across the American front line to crash among friends.

Close support was Herb's mission number thirty-five on April 16, 1945.

Back at base, Herb marched into the operations tent to collect his aluminum name strip from the board. The operations officer ran a line through Herb's name in the blue personnel notebook, writing "TDC" for "tour of duty completed" after it. April 16, 1945, was Herb's personal "Victory in Europe" Day.

★ ★ ★

Back in the States in 1945, victory was a mixed bag for John. His neighborhood in Cincinnati was festooned with "Double V for Victory" stickers, and Lieutenant Leahr, the decorated Negro fighter pilot, was a celebrity in the black community. Even white newspapers took note. "Flying Yank Returns Home After Fifty Missions," crowed the *Cincinnati Call-Post*. On the other hand, the AAF was still resisting the second V for Victory.

The AAF just didn't know what to do with Negro aviators. The top brass didn't want any additional black fighter squadrons, but the political pressure was relentless to widen the opportunities for blacks in the AAF. In 1943, the AAF announced a new experiment in segregated aviation—medium bombers. The 477th Colored Bombardment Group (Medium) turned out to be as awkward as its name.

A segregated bomber group was an even worse idea than a segregated fighter group. At least fighters required only one segregated flying school for pilots. Segregated bombers would need segregated schools for bombardiers, navigators, and air gunners, along with pilots and copilots. The 477th Colored Bombardment Group (Medium) began as the usual segregated mess—inefficient, uncoordinated, and deeply insulting. After all the required training, personnel, and B-25 medium bombers were united, the 477th was sent to an AAF airfield outside Detroit to get organized. From there, things went from bad to worse. The 477th was moved and moved again. It was moved thirty-eight times before it landed at a rural airfield in Indiana called Freeman Field.

Wild rumors about the 477th were flying around Tuskegee AAF in Alabama when John reported there for duty in March 1945. Lieutenant Leahr had returned to Tuskegee, Alabama, in a hopeful state of mind. He'd been selected for another AAF experiment—training experienced black pilots to become flight instructors. John and his classmates would take over the

training of black B-25 pilots for new segregated bomber groups. But first, John had to learn how to fly the two-engine B-25 himself.

That was fun. John already had more than 750 flying hours (including 400 in combat) in single-seat fighters. Getting his "multiengine" rating wasn't hard. Within weeks, he was comfortable at the controls of a B-25J. It was a two-engine bomber designed for a crew of five or six and a bomb load of 3,000 pounds, but without bombs, long-range tanks, or other crew, the B-25J flew like a fighter, to John's delight. The others in John's multiengine class were veteran Red Tails, and they raced their B-25Js at low altitude and high speed across the flat Alabama countryside. At those times, John thought the AAF was a wonderful place to be a hot pilot in a fast machine.

The AAF, however, was still a difficult place for African Americans in 1945. In April, the AAF's experiment in segregated bombers collapsed in what became known as the "Freeman Field Mutiny." The white colonel commanding the 477th collided head on with his black officers. Freeman Field had two officers' clubs: one for whites and one for blacks. The colonel

Home safe: Wearing his A-2 leather pilot's jacket, John cut an incredibly cool figure on the streets of Cincinnati while on home furlough after his return from Italy. Unfortunately, John found out that there were still Americans who couldn't tolerate the sight of a black man in officer's bars and pilot's wings.

drew up a formal order forbidding black officers from entering the white club, marching every black officer on the base into his office to sign it. Threatened with court-martial for "mutiny," 101 of them still refused. The next morning, the "mutineers" were flown in transport planes to Fort Knox in Kentucky, where they were taken into custody by fully armed infantry in armored vehicles.

Eventually, cooler heads prevailed, but not before twelve senators, four congressmen, the White House, and a young black lawyer for the NAACP named Thurgood Marshall came to the defense of the mutineers. (Much later, Thurgood Marshall would become the first African American justice on the U.S. Supreme Court.) The mutineers were sent back to Freeman Field to continue training. Both officers' clubs were shut down. The 477th Colored Bombardment Group (Medium) was still training when the war ended.

John missed the Freeman Field Mutiny. He would hear all about it from other Tuskegees, but in June 1945, John was in Kennedy Army Hospital in Memphis, Tennessee. He was there for a goiter operation. A goiter is an enlargement of the thyroid glands in the neck. John's condition had nothing to do with Freeman Field, the AAF, or his war service, but once the Tuskegee flight surgeon diagnosed his problem, surgery was recommended. With John's arrival, there were four black officers at Kennedy Hospital. Casualties were still pouring in from battlefields in Europe and the Pacific, but the army put the four black officers into their own hospital ward. The army would not mix officers and enlisted men in a hospital ward, let alone blacks and whites. One of the other black officers was a Tuskegee pilot, but John was the only air combat veteran. All four quickly became friends.

John's goiter operation was a success, but he remained at Kennedy under doctor's orders to take it easy. His new friends had a different prescription. What John needed, they said, was home cooking and a few beers. They knew where to get both. They'd made friends with a black pharmacist in Memphis, a Mr. William Martin, who liked to entertain colored servicemen, especially officers, at his house. If they could take the city bus to Mr. Martin's pharmacy at closing time, he would take them home, feed them up, and have them back at the hospital before curfew. The Memphis bus line, however, was segregated. John found that annoying, but the thought of home cooking was irresistible. To get to Mr. Martin's pharmacy, they would have to change buses in downtown Memphis. John thought that would be tiring.

The four black officers rode a late-afternoon bus downtown. The army required convalescing patients to wear their dress uniforms outside hospital grounds. John was particularly elegant in his pilot's "crush" hat, silver wings, and discreet row of combat service ribbons. The officers got off to change buses downtown, and suddenly a drunk—an aggressive, loud, foul-talking white drunk—accosted them.

He was a thug if there ever was one, John remembered. The drunk stopped and said, "I'll be damned. Look at these niggers. And nigger officers." The drunk focused his eyes more closely and said, "Two of them got wings on. Damn, I've killed a lot of niggers, but I never killed any nigger officers."

The officers ignored the drunk as he yanked at their jackets and poked at their insignia. A crowd gathered. John waited for someone to tell the drunk to leave those service boys alone. But the drunk was determined to have a little fun, and there was nothing John or the other three could do to stop him. They were officers and gentlemen, but they were invalids, unable to defend themselves or even to run away. The drunk was enjoying himself. The crowd grew larger. A police car pulled to the curb and a white policeman got out, demanding, "What's going on here?" The drunk told him, "Nothing. I'm just gonna kill some niggers. I've killed a lot of niggers, but I never killed a nigger officer." The policeman got back into the squad car and drove away.

This was the final insult. John had fought the Germans overseas and had survived. Now he was about to be lynched in downtown Memphis by an American drunk while an American crowd stood by. Suddenly a white sailor pushed through the crowd, also demanding, "What's going on here?" The drunk gave him the same old racist rant. The sailor asked, "What did they do to you?" The drunk admitted, "They didn't do nothing to me. I just don't like 'em." And the sailor said, "I don't like 'em either, but when they don't do anything to me, I don't bother them." Then the white sailor said to John, "Where you boys going?" Just then a bus pulled up. It didn't matter where the bus was going. It was their bus. The sailor eased them through the crowd and onto the bus. A navy enlisted man had just rescued four army officers. It was race, not rank, that mattered.

John never got to eat Mr. Martin's home cooking. Back at the hospital, he called Tuskegee Army Airfield. The operations officer was a friend and classmate. "I'm up here at the hospital in Memphis and I almost got lynched," John explained. "I can't stay here any longer. How soon can you have an airplane up here to pick me up?" His friend said, "I'll have one up there for you at eight o'clock in the morning." And John said, "Send it."

John signed himself out of the hospital that night and in the morning caught a B-25J back to Tuskegee. He finished his instructor's training course, but that was the end of John's plans for a military career. His uniform, his pilot's wings, and his combat service ribbons couldn't protect him from a racist drunk in downtown Memphis. John knew that the army would not have lifted a finger to defend him if John had punched the drunk out and been arrested. John wanted out of the South and out of the segregated AAF as soon as possible.

A month before, May 8, 1945, had been V-E Day—Victory in Europe Day. Less than two months later came V-J Day—Victory over Japan Day—on August 15, 1945. There was no Double V for Victory Day.

Both John and Herb were demobilized—released to civilian life again—by the AAF in early 1946. They were still fifty-one years away from shaking hands. In between, Herb and John had their civilian lives to live—careers, education, romance, marriage, children, grandchildren, success, some failures, a few heartbreaks, and then a raft of late-breaking news about their service in World War II.

At the start of his tour, Herb swore to the operations officer that his nameplate would not end up in the trash can along with those of the other dead and missing crews. In 1945, Herb took his nameplate home. Sixty years later, he still had it.

Mission Debriefing

The old neighborhood had certainly changed in seventy-five years, but John and Herb found bits and pieces of their childhood everywhere as we drove around. I was at the wheel, the baby boomer "kid" chauffeuring two old friends who'd grown up on these streets but on different sides of the color line. North Avondale Elementary was still there, although the old mansion had been torn down long ago and replaced with a larger, purpose-built school. Herb and John wondered what had happened to the big boulder on the school lawn. They remembered climbing all over that boulder. The school's May Day celebrations had been held on the lawn right next to it. All the neighborhood kids had sworn that it was a meteorite, fallen straight out of the sky and onto the school lawn. That didn't sound very likely to Herb and John now, but where had the boulder gone? I pulled to the curb outside the school while John and Herb compared memory to the present layout. They must have dug the boulder up when they built the new school, Herb and John decided.

We went looking for Herb's old house. Even after seventy-five

The Leahr family gathers in 1994 to celebrate the ninety-ninth birthday of Robert Leahr, John's father, who sits on the sofa with his second wife, Pauline. His father remarried after John's mother, Rosezelia, died in 1965. In the crowd are his children, grandchildren, nieces, nephews, and their spouses. John is in the center, in the striped tie. Robert Leahr lived to be 106.

through top secret Nazi reports on production, transport, and energy. They tried to count the dead, the wounded, and those made homeless by the bombing. It all went into a top secret debriefing called the "U.S. Strategic Bombing Survey" in September 1945. It was startling reading then, and, after it was declassified in 1967, still startling reading today.

The Allied strategic bombing campaign against Hitler's war machine had not gone according to plan. The bombing survey concluded that the massive air campaign had been "decisive"; that is, strategic bombing had been key to Hitler's defeat, but not in the way that the AAF bomber generals had expected. For one, most of their bombs had missed their targets. The AAF defined a hit as a bomb landing within a thousand feet of its intended target. The survey concluded that only 20 percent fell that close.

That reopened an old argument about bombing accuracy between the British bomber generals of the RAF and the American bomber generals of the AAF. Early in the war, the RAF Bomber Command switched to bombing by night after heavy losses to German fighters and flak gunners by day. Bombing by night was safer for the raiders, but the RAF had to give up on pinpoint accuracy. Night targets had to be large, easy to find, and impossible to hide. Cities were perfect night bombing targets. The Luftwaffe had already learned this during the Battle of Britain. When RAF fighters cut up the German bombers by day, the Luftwaffe turned to night bombing raids. Hitting an airplane factory or a military airfield at night from 20,000 feet was next to impossible. London at night was impossible to miss. The RAF strategic bombing goal was similarly blunt— smash up German cities, destroy factories, and demoralize the civilian work force.

When the United States entered the bombing war in 1942, the

AAF bomber generals rejected night bombing. They believed instead that large, self-protecting formations of B-17 "Flying Fortresses" could fight their way into German territory in broad daylight and blast key industrial targets with precision. So the Allies divided the strategic air war into night and day. The RAF bombed by night and the AAF bombed by day. It took nearly four years, 2.7 million tons of bombs, and the loss of 40,000 Allied aircraft before the Nazi war machine collapsed. Allied bombing of German cities and towns killed at least 300,000 civilians and left 7.5 million people homeless. (Luftwaffe bombers killed 60,000 British civilians during the Battle of Britain.) The Nazi army was finally beaten in May 1945, but had the strategic bombing campaign delivered the knockout blow?

The bombing survey said that the AAF bombing generals never expected victory by strategic bombing alone. The air generals expected the ground armies—the Americans and British from the West and the Soviet Red Army from the East—to overrun the German army in its homeland. But the air generals thought strategic bombing would tip the scales in the ground war. The bombing survey concluded that the air generals had been right on two counts. Their planes tore up the railroads that supplied the German military, and they dried up the German oil supply. In the Battle of the Bulge, German Panzer divisions ran out of fuel. On the Eastern Front, 1,200 German tanks were pushed into place without fuel to stop the advancing Red Army at the Vistula River. Unable to move, tanks and crews were easily picked off.

Yet the strategic bombing campaigns had little lasting effect on most other aspects of German war production, according to the report. Tanks, guns, and military equipment poured from German war plants until the last months of the war. The survey discovered that the number of German aircraft produced had actually increased through 1944 and into early 1945, including 1,400 of the deadly new ME-262 fighter jets. Yet the Luftwaffe was without enough fuel and experienced pilots to fly the jets, thanks to the relentless hammering of oil refineries by Allied bombers.

That's what Herb, John, and the rest of the Fifteenth Air Force were doing in Italy. In looking over the lists of targets that they attacked, I could see their squadrons going back, time after time, to destroy synthetic oil refineries and railroad marshaling yards. Neither John nor Herb chose his targets or his missions. In their personal war aims, going home was their decisive event in World War II.

The two most amazing things about Herb's career as a B-17 pilot took fifty years to catch up with him. It was 1997 before Herb and John met again. It was 1995 before Herb learned that his best friend from bomber pilot training, Lyle Pearson, was not dead! Reading a veterans' newsletter, Herb stumbled across a short news item about Lyle C. Pearson, a former B-17 pilot and former national commander of the Disabled American Veterans. The newsletter said Pearson was living in North Mankato, Minnesota. Herb called information and found a phone number for L. C. Pearson in North Mankato. When Lyle came to the phone, Herb almost burst into tears.

On December 29, 1944, Herb saw Lyle's plane knocked from the sky over the Brenner Pass. Now, fifty years later, Lyle was on the phone calmly telling Herb how he and four other crew members had survived the crash and then four months in a *stalag*, a German prisoner-of-war (POW) camp.

The plane exploded before his crew could bail out, Lyle said, but the blast tossed everyone at the front of the B-17—the pilot, copilot,

★ 14()

navigator, and bombardier—through the Plexiglas nose into midair. Lyle didn't remember the blast. He was knocked out and woke up to find himself tumbling through the air. Instinctively, Lyle pulled his parachute release cord. So did his bombardier and the tail gunner (who jumped from the breakaway tail section), but his copilot, Sam Wheeler, was in worse trouble. He'd been blown out of the plane without his parachute. Freefalling in the debris, Wheeler was struck in the chest by a loose parachute pack. He grabbed it and managed to hook it on and release it just in time.

Lyle's navigator, Arthur Frechette, was not that lucky. Yet Frechette survived. Later, Lyle sent Herb a copy of a June 1945 newspaper story that documented one of the amazing survival stories of World War II. A reporter from the army newspaper, *Stars & Stripes,* had interviewed Frechette in the army hospital just after his release from a German POW camp. Frechette told the reporter that he had been wrestling with the forward escape hatch when the plane exploded. Like the others, Frechette was blown into space, but the navigator had a parachute securely fastened to his chest harness. Like the others, he was knocked out by the blast. Unlike the others, Frechette didn't wake up. Unconscious, he fell more than four miles toward the mountains below. "I came to a few seconds before I hit the side of the mountain," Frechette told the reporter. "I knew my chute wasn't open. I guess I resigned myself more or less to dying, but I grabbed for my ripcord."

The reporter described what happened next. "His [Frechette's] hand was still on the ripcord handle when he hit the snow. The snow was only a few feet deep where he landed, but the mountain sloped away in a 45-degree angle and the dazed navigator began rolling as soon as he hit. About 100 yards away, he dropped off a four-foot ledge, rolled a short distance and stopped." Frechette had broken his right arm, crushed his left kneecap, and severely sprained his right ankle. He told the reporter, "I didn't know if I was dead or if I'd been unconscious for a long time so I looked up to see what time it was. There was my [bomb] group still heading for the target, just a little ways past me. I don't think I ever felt so lonely in my life."

Somewhere in that high-flying B-17 formation, Herb and his crew were continuing toward the secondary target. Frechette was captured by a German soldier and carried down the mountain on a straw-covered farmer's sled. After receiving medical attention, he joined Lyle and the other survivors as prisoners of war. But Herb never heard any of this. For the next fifty years, Herb believed that Lyle had died before his eyes.

How could that be? How did Herb miss the news that his best friend in the AAF was not dead but a prisoner? The simplest explanation is that all battles are confusing and messy, especially to those in the fighting. The end of World War II in Europe was particularly messy. By V-E Day, Herb was on a troopship bound for Boston Harbor when Lyle's POW camp in Austria was finally liberated by American troops.

The end of the war against Japan—V-J Day—found Herb back in Ohio, stationed at Wright Army Airfield near Dayton. Peace gave Herb his old civilian life back. Honorably discharged from the AAF in 1946, Herb discovered his talents as a salesman, first selling ads for a big AM radio station in Cincinnati and later switching to selling commercial real estate. Peace also gave Herb his personal life back again. He married Phyllis Dautch Juvelier in 1957, becoming a stepfather to Susie, and then the father of Jeff and Doug. Then came a divorce and then remarriage in 1993 to Carol Thies, making Herb stepfather to Pam, Bill, Christi, David, and Marni. By then, it had been fifty years since his last B-17 mission. Herb suddenly found himself thinking more and more about the war. Why had he survived when so many had not? What had happened to the others? That curiosity led him to the newsletter item about Lyle Pearson. Two years later, Herb spotted the newspaper story about the Tuskegee reunion that led him to John Leahr.

Back in 1945, peace gave John little to celebrate. After his near lynching in Memphis, John was determined to get out of the AAF. The other veteran Tuskegee pilots tried to talk John out of quitting. You should take a regular officer's commission in the peacetime army, the Tuskegees urged him. Big changes are coming, they promised. The Jim Crow air force is doomed, they said—we'll be the ones to bust this wide open. And they were right, although it would be a hard road to walk for the Tuskegee officers who endured the transition.

Two events opened the way. Congress gave the "air" generals independence, making the U.S. Army Air Forces into a separate U.S. Air Force in 1947. A year later, Jim Crow was drummed out of the American military. On July 26, 1948, President Harry S. Truman signed Executive Order 9981, declaring that henceforth, "there shall be equality of treatment and opportunity for all persons in the armed services without regard to race, color, religion, or national origin."

But change did not happen overnight. The regular army, for example, did not abolish its last segregated unit until 1954. Inside the new U.S. Air Force, legal (that is, de jure) segregation was dead, but outside the gates of many air bases in the South and West, Jim Crow was alive and perfectly legal. Black pilots flew F-86 Sabre jets in integrated combat squadrons during the Korean War. They came home to assignments in American states where local segregation laws were in full force. Their base commanders told the black pilots to respect local racial customs outside the perimeter fence. It wasn't until 1963 that the secretary of defense finally ordered base commanders to insist on full civil rights for black servicemen and women off base.

For the Tuskegee pilots who gritted their teeth and followed military careers, the rewards were real but hard won. B. O. Davis, Jr., as always, took the lead. Immediately after V-E Day, Colonel Davis was ordered home to pick up the pieces after the Freeman Field "Mutiny." Davis consolidated the AAF's remaining segregated bomber and fighter squadrons into a single all-black aviation unit, the 477th Composite Group, based in Columbus, Ohio. When President Truman ordered the armed services to desegregate, Colonel Davis was called to the Pentagon to draft an air force integration plan and wrote the orders that dispersed the 477th, the last of the Tuskegee units.

For his leadership role, Davis was made a one-star brigadier general in 1954, a two-star major general in 1959, and a three-star lieutenant general in 1965. Davis retired in 1970 but was recalled to the White House in 1998 by President Clinton, who made him a full four-star general, the highest peacetime rank in the U.S. Armed Forces. General Davis died on the Fourth of July 2002, at age eighty-nine. Other Tuskegees had high-flying U.S. Air Force careers. A Tuskegee flying school classmate of John's, Daniel "Chappie" James, was the first African American on active duty to reach the rank of four-star general in 1975.

In the early twenty-first century, the U.S. military is widely regarded as the country's most "colorblind" institution. The struggle for racial equality in the military was fought behind closed doors in peacetime and in combat during the Korean and Vietnam wars. It was an amazing transformation in American thinking.

Race was not the only issue that the U.S military had to rethink. Vietnam forced the armed forces to reconsider the role of women in war. More than 210,000 American women served in uniform during World War II, especially in army auxiliary and medical units (including 6,520 black women in the Women's Army Medical Corps and 500 in the Army Nurses Corps). Unsurprisingly, the Army Air Corps resisted women pilots almost as vehemently as it resisted black ones. In 1930, an internal Air Corps report declared that women were "too high strung for wartime flying" and that training women as ferry pilots was "totally unfeasible." By late 1942, a shortage of ferry pilots made female ones feasible. The air generals grumbled, but women were allowed to sign on as civilian Women Air Service Pilots (WASPs). While training, delivering new aircraft, or testing repaired ones, thirty-eight WASP fliers were killed in the line of duty during World War II. The civilians were not entitled to military burial. Sometimes, the WASP fliers had to pass the hat to collect money to bury one of their own.

That attitude has changed. In the early twenty-first century, American women serve in a wide range of military assignments, including helicopter, transport, and even fighter pilots. Women pilots are supposedly banned from front-line combat stations, but modern war is no respecter of lines. During the first Gulf War in 1991, Major Marie T. Rossi was killed while leading her Chinook helicopter medical evacuation squadron. Her headstone at Arlington National Cemetery describes Major Rossi as America's "First Female Combat Commander to Fly into Battle."

For those caught up in History, change can be hard to see in their own time. But look at pictures of American soldiers, sailors, and pilots during the 2003 invasion of Iraq. Those pictures show all kinds of

Americans—all races, both genders, all religions. Then look at pictures of Herb's bomber squadron in 1944. It's all white guys. Look at pictures of John's fighter group just down the road. It's all black guys. The only women stationed near either airfield were army nurses and visiting Red Cross "doughnut girls." John remembered the first time in 1944 that an all-white Red Cross "mobile field canteen" showed up at the all-black Ramitelli airfield. History was made when a white American Red Cross worker handed a pastry to a black American fighter pilot. They were good doughnuts, John recalled.

That doughnut now belongs to History with a big "H." Living through history with a small "h," John found the postwar years frustrating. "I was bitter," John told me. Honorably discharged in 1946, he went home to pick up his civilian life where he'd left it four years before in Cincinnati. "I came back to the same old thing," John said. "Nothing had changed."

If anything, things were worse. By the time John got home, his old job in the foundry at Wright Aero was gone. War plants were shutting down or scaling back by squeezing out women and "temporary" Negro war workers to make room for the returning "boys"—the white boys. Flying for an airline was out of the question. (The first black pilot was not hired by a major American passenger airline until 1963.) John did take advantage of the educational benefits offered to all veterans under the postwar "GI Bill of Rights." Uncle Sam paid for John's return to the University of Cincinnati, where he avoided the Elementary Education department and graduated in 1948 with a degree in political science and economics. John left UC with a diploma, no job prospects, and a fiancée, Geneva Sechrest. John and Geneva married in 1949.

Once married, John and Geneva ran head-on into the postwar housing shortage. The housing crunch was doubly bad for black veterans and their families. Their house hunting was limited to black neighborhoods, mostly in overcrowded inner-city districts. John and Geneva ended up across the river in the black section of Covington, Kentucky. Every morning, John crossed the Ohio River for a two-hour drive north to Wright-Patterson Air Force Base, where he was a civilian clerk. John wasn't happy about the drive or the job. "I couldn't get a job in Cincinnati," he recalled. "I was lucky enough to get one at Wright-Patterson."

President Truman's desegregation order also outlawed racial discrimination in civilian hiring for the military. As a veteran, a decorated pilot, and a college graduate, John was a prime candidate for a civilian career with a desegregated U.S. Air Force. But after four years at Wright-Patterson, John was still a low-level clerk and likely to remain one forever. He'd hit a new kind of color line, a "glass ceiling," a de facto limit on how high a black man could rise in the Air Force bureaucracy in the 1950s. It was a pattern he'd see all his working life.

Never a man to sit around and wait for history to catch up, John left his government job to try his hand at small business. He decided to become an undertaker. Preachers, doctors, and funeral directors had always been the pillars of the black community. John went back to school again to become a licensed mortician, only to discover that without a huge pile of cash or a father in the funeral business, it was next to impossible to break in on his own.

John tried big business. He returned in 1953 to his old prewar employer, Wright Aero, which had been bought up by General Electric. It was a boom time again in the airplane business. GE Aircraft Engines was cranking out turbojets for the military and then for new civilian jet airliners. John was no longer in the foundry department, but he soon found himself up to his elbows in toxic liquid mercury in the jet engine testing bays. After six years in industry, John tried finance. He went into the stock market, becoming the first African American to pass Ohio's license exams and the first to be named a vice president of an Ohio brokerage firm. Eventually, John became a senior personnel administrator for Cincinnati Gas & Electric, one of the few African Americans at such a high level in the company. But he rose no higher. He'd hit another glass ceiling. All his working life, John had been a pioneer, and yet when he retired in 1983, he felt worn out by the resilience of the color line.

John also had a full personal life—as husband to Geneva for forty-four years until her death in 1993, as father to John W. and Arthur Ray, and as grandfather to Robert Louis Leahr. John was active in the Boy Scouts, the Red Cross (in partial payback for the doughnuts in Italy), and the Citizens Committee on Youth. He was an elder at his neighborhood Presbyterian church and co-chair of his neighborhood community council.

And John was a founding member in 1972 of the Tuskegee Airmen, the first black air force veterans' group. The country, it seemed to John, had forgotten that an all-black segregated air force had ever existed. Young people, especially black children, worried him most of all. By the 1970s, the civil rights movement had come—and some said gone—and African American kids either did not know or didn't want to know about the way things were before. A segregated fighter squadron was not glorious in their eyes. It reminded them of the old humiliations forced on black people. But John felt that kids—black and white—needed to see the funny old uniforms, the antique airplanes, and the serious young black men who'd gone to war as Tuskegee Airmen. That became John's never-ending mission.

The Tuskegee mission tied in with John's other great interest, travel. Once Geneva retired from teaching, they were free to hit the road. They took ocean cruises to warm places and long overland trips in their motor home. Traveling south of the Ohio River was no longer the Jim Crow ordeal that John remembered from his AAF days. Public accommodations—restaurants, motels, and bathrooms—were open to all, at least on the main tourist routes. No longer did black travelers in the American South have to go around back and buy sandwiches at the kitchen door from the cook.

After Geneva's death, John still traveled, alone or with old friends. He hadn't piloted an airplane in decades, but a long highway cruise was almost as good. Stopping after a day on the road, John liked to thumb through local phonebooks, searching for lost Tuskegees or other black servicemen he'd met during the war. And so it was one evening in 1995 that John stopped for the night in Winston-Salem, North Carolina, and suddenly remembered George White. He had been one of the other black officers convalescing at Kennedy Army Hospital in June 1945 when John arrived for his operation. John hadn't seen George White since. Now fifty years later, John recalled Lieutenant White talking about his hometown of Winston-Salem. It was a common name, but after telephoning several "G. Whites," John got lucky. A young woman answered and listened politely to John's long explanation about being an ex-army officer who'd been in Kennedy Army Hospital in 1945 with a Lieutenant George White from Winston-Salem. Would this be his residence? There was a long silence. "You'd better talk to my mom," she said.

Mrs. White said yes, this was George White's home, but her husband had passed ten years before. John said he was terribly sorry and apologized for intruding. Please wait, said Mrs. White. She had something that John should see. Was he in town long? Just overnight, John said. Well, then we must have breakfast, said Mrs. White. She gave him directions to meet her at the best breakfast spot in town.

Next morning, Mrs. White and her daughter showed up for breakfast with a manila envelope. She told John that she'd almost thrown it away when she'd cleaned out her husband's desk a few months after his death. Yet she'd had a feeling that someone might come looking for these things one day. Mrs. White emptied out a small pile of tattered black-and-white snapshots onto the tabletop. The photos had been taken in front of Kennedy General Hospital in June 1945. Here was her husband, Mrs. White said, pointing to a dapper young officer in a neatly pressed khaki summer uniform. And here you are, she said.

The man could fly: Lt. John H. Leahr, combat veteran, outside Kennedy Army Hospital in Memphis with Lt. George White, June 1944.

Despite the June heat, Lieutenant Leahr is wearing his dark winter uniform. John's head is cocked to one side. His arms are akimbo, a hand on each hip. Even without the silver wings and the crushed pilot's hat, there is no question about which officer is the fighter pilot. Lieutenant

John Leahr looks confident enough to fly without an airplane. If you could declare victory in a picture, this is John's victory, no matter what happened afterward. Sometimes the big picture takes time to become clear.

In 1997, John and Herb met again. John told me what he remembered of the ceremony that day honoring the Red Tails on Cincinnati's Fountain Square and of the private reception that he helped organize afterward in a nearby hotel. John recalled looking across the room and seeing this white guy about his age cutting through the crowd. The stranger grabbed John by the hand, asked if he'd flown with the Fifteenth Air Force in Italy. "I thought Herb was trying to sell me something," John remembered. "I was sure he was an insurance salesman."

It took Herb and John months to become real friends. First they had to eat lunch and meet each other's families. Then they had to compare notes on their common memories and unravel their separate lives. They matched up pieces of memory: the old neighborhood, growing up during the Depression, Pearl Harbor, and Wright Aero. Then came surviving Air Cadet training, surviving flight school, and surviving Italy.

Some pieces of common memory had different shapes. Herb remembered the neighborhood movie houses where he'd spent Saturday mornings watching shoot-em-up Westerns. John said that blacks weren't allowed in the neighborhood movie houses. He'd seen his Westerns downtown from the colored balcony or in black neighborhood theaters. Herb couldn't believe how close they'd come to meeting so many times. Why, said Herb, they must have been standing next to each other at Wright Aero. "Well, if you were standing next to me then," said John, "you must have been hot, because it was hotter than hell in the foundry." When John told Herb about his near lynching in Memphis, Herb's mouth fell open in shock and in shame.

But John and Herb did become real friends. It was something they could not have imagined when they were young. Now they were old, and they started keeping tabs on each other by phone. They saved up awful jokes for each other. Then Herb unearthed Miss Pitchell's 1928 class photo. The portrait stunned them. It was one thing to trace their lives through time, seeing how close they'd been without meeting. It was another to see how they started out at age eight, standing next to each other.

John had been speaking about the Tuskegees for nearly twenty years to school and youth groups. Now he asked if Herb would like to come along. Herb said he'd be honored. Herb's stepson had their class photo blown up into a giant transparent slide so it could be projected onto a screen. Their first joint speaking engagement was at a racially mixed suburban elementary school. Kids can be a tough audience, especially for two old men come to talk about an old war. But John's a great speaker, Herb recalled, and he soon had their attention. Then it was Herb's turn. He spoke about flying B-17s, about the Red Tail escorts, and about inviting himself to the Tuskegee reunion, where he met John Leahr for the second time. Then Herb put on the projector slide of Miss Pitchell's class. The kids went totally silent.

"That's me," Herb said. "And right next to me, that's John." The children looked from the old photo to the men standing before them. For the first time, they actually saw John and Herb, saw them as kids, as young men, and as old friends. The kids were speechless.

The "John & Herb Show" was already picking up steam when I first caught up with them in 2000. They'd presented it more than a dozen times at local schools, colleges, and business groups. They'd been written up in the Cincinnati newspapers. I'd heard about them through my friend Chot, who told me about his amazing brother-in-law. I came to Cincinnati to write a feature story about Herb and John for an aviation magazine. Once my story appeared, the pace quickened. Their story

In the early twenty-first century, the story of John and Herb, third-grade classmates and air battle companions, began attracting national attention from newspapers, magazines, and network television. In 2003, Harvard University awarded John and Herb a gold medal for "promoting racial understanding."

was written up in national newspapers and magazines. They were on the national TV news and on cable history channels. In 2003, Harvard University flew Herb and John to Cambridge, Massachusetts. They gave their speech to Harvard undergraduates and came home with a Harvard gold medal for services on behalf of "racial understanding." The speaking engagements and the honors kept coming. In 2006, John and Herb turned eighty-six, still in good health and still giving their talks, although their families were pressing them not to overdo it.

I've been to several of their talks, but I remember the first one clearly. It taught me my first lesson about age and mirrors. I started off by thinking that someone had made a mistake in the booking arrangements. John and Herb had been invited to address a community college class that was studying World War II. That sounded promising. I imagined a class of young college students soaking up a great historical lesson. But once we set out in John's Cadillac, I had a closer look at the invitation. We were going to a class at the "Institute for Learning in Retirement." Herb and John were going to address a class of senior citizens. What was the point of that?

The point is that age is a distorted mirror. Looking back, everything is closer than it appears. The retirement institute students that day were senior citizens, but they were "only" in their sixties and early seventies. They'd been teenagers at the end of the war, too young to fight or work in war industries. They'd lived World War II through the war stories brought home by fathers, uncles, aunts, and older brothers. Today in class, these senior citizens would be teenagers again, listening to John and Herb talk about their War. I was in the back of the classroom with my notebook, and when John began talking, I suddenly felt eight years old again. I was sitting in my Aunt Catherine's kitchen on a late summer night, listening to grownups talk about things they rarely talked about. My Uncle Jim was dredging up what he remembered about being blown up at the Battle of the Bulge. He'd lost his helmet, Jim recalled, and kept asking the medics for it until someone finally slammed a spare one on his head to shut him up. Then Jim didn't want to talk about the Battle of the Bulge anymore. That was the War as I heard it.

John began with a video segment from a TV documentary on the Tuskegees. He talked about the Tuskegees' struggle against the AAF top brass, against racism everywhere, and against the Germans at 30,000 feet. John talked about the fighter war, about the escort missions, and about surviving through skill, luck, and prayer. John told them about his near lynching in Memphis. The audience groaned.

Herb told them about the bomber war. He told them about the nametags in the operations tent and how the dead and the missing went into the trash can to make room for replacements. Herb reached into his pocket and held up a battered aluminum strip with "Heilbrun" painted on it in white. He'd brought it home after thirty-five missions. "In all those missions, I was never under fighter attack," Herb said. "If it weren't for men like John Leahr, I wouldn't be here. So that's one reason I like John Leahr. Actually, that's the main reason I like John Leahr." The audience laughed.

Herb told them about his homecoming in 1945, about meeting John all those years later and about learning how different their lives had been, with race making much of the difference. Then Herb turned on the projector and showed them Miss Pitchell's class. The students gasped. Then they laughed. Herb was right. The picture never missed.

At the end, Herb and John had one request. "Don't forget us," Herb said.

PHOTO CREDITS

RESOURCES

The danger in finding out more about World War II is in getting swamped by how much there is to find. Even small school or branch libraries will have bookcases stuffed with World War II history along with war novels, films, and even poetry. Probably the best method is to start with a narrow question and see where it takes you. This is not foolproof. Starting with the Tuskegee Airmen can take you places you never expected to visit. But that may not be so bad after all. Here are a few of the places I visited while researching this book.

For the Tuskegees, try the following:

Stanley Sandler, *Segregated Skies* (Washington, D.C.: Smithsonian Institution, 1992). This is the most "authoritative" history, meaning that the author was an academic historian who worked by the strict rules of historical research, relying on primary sources whenever possible. These are reports and accounts written at the time the events were happening. Memory changes the past. People forget how confusing great events can be, and when they sit down later to look back, everything seems clearer.

Charles E. Francis and Adolph Caso, *The Tuskegee Airmen* (Branden Publishing, 1997). Francis wrote the first "popular" book on the Tuskegees in 1956, after interviewing many of the Tuskegees while their memories of the war were still fresh. This is the fourth edition, updated and revised by Adolph Caso. It has a great chronology of Tuskegee AAF history.

Lynn M. Homan and Thomas Reilly, *Black Knights* (Gretna, La.: Pelican Publishing, 2001). Again, more eyewitness accounts supplement the official history.

For a comprehensive list of books and other source materials about the Tuskegees and African Americans in the U.S. Armed Forces, go to the Web site of the Senior Noncommissioned Office Academy Library: www.au.af.mil/au/aul/school/sncoa/tusk.htm#book.

For an overview of African American experiences in the military: Morris J. MacGregor, *Integration of the Armed Forces, 1940–1965* (Washington, D.C.: Center for Military History, 1981). Also available online at www.army.mil/CMH-PG/books/integration/IAF-fm.htm. Alan B. Osur, *Blacks in the Armed Forces During World War II* (Washington, D.C.: Office of Air Force History, 1977).

For the air war in general:

Edward Jablonski, *Air War* (Garden City, N.Y.: Doubleday, 1979).

For the B-17 specifically, try Jablonski's earlier book:

Edward Jablonski, *Flying Fortress* (Garden City, N.Y.: Doubleday, 1965).

For the official history:

Kit C. Carter, *Combat Chronology, 1941–1945* (Washington, D.C.: Center for Air Force History, 1991). Also available online at www.airforcehistory.hq.af.mil/PopTopics/chron/title.htmwww.airforcehistory.hq.af.mil/PopTopics/chron/title.htm.

For Herb Heilbrun's 301st Bomb Group, try to find a copy of Kenneth P. Werrell, *"Who Fears?": The 301st in War and Peace* (Dallas: Taylor Publishing, 1991).

These books are going to be hard to find, but they were my main sources for the history of de facto segregation in Cincinnati schools:

Thomas Paul Kessen, *Segregation in Cincinnati Public Education: The Nineteenth Century Experience* (Ann Arbor, Mich.: University Microfilms, 1973).

W. A. Montgomery, *Racial History of the Cincinnati and Suburban Public Schools,* plaintiff's exhibit, 1982, copy at Education Department, Public Library of Cincinnati and Hamilton County, Cincinnati, Ohio.

For the air war at the movies:

The best—and so far the only—dramatic movie about the Tuskegees is *The Tuskegee Airmen* (1995), starring Laurence Fishburne, Allen Payne, Malcolm-Jamal Warner, and Courtney Vance. PBS did a nonfiction documentary (2003), also called *The Tuskegee Airmen,* narrated by Ossie Davis.

It's harder to choose the best movie about B-17s. *Memphis Belle* (1990), starring Matthew Modine and Harry Connick, Jr., was a melodramatic remake of *The Memphis Belle: A Story of a Flying Fortress,* a documentary made for the government during World War II by the famous movie director William Wyler. The other choice for a B-17 drama would be *Twelve O'Clock High* (1949), starring Gregory Peck and Dean Jagger.

For primary source material, go to the U.S. Government Printing Office Web site to see if you live near a library that belongs to the Federal Depository Library Program (FDLP): www.gpoaccess.gov/fdlp.html. Scattered across the United States, FDLP libraries have copies of nearly everything issued by the federal government during World War II, including instruction books for flying a B-17 ("Pilot Training Manual for the Flying Fortress, AAF Manual No. 50-13") or a P-51 ("Pilot Training Manual for the Mustang, AAF Manual 51-127-5"). It's the next best thing to flying one yourself.

Best World War II Web sites:

The best all-around, nongovernment Web site for World War II history is "The World War II Timeline" created by Steve Schoenherr, a history professor at the University of San Diego. It links to everything World War II—special libraries, government archives, veterans' groups, picture sources, documentaries, reading lists, and so on. It's at www.history.sandiego.edu/gen/ww2timeline.

The Smithsonian National Air & Space Museum in Washington, D.C., and northern Virginia (www.nasm.si.edu/) has many World War II aircraft, but the best World War II aviation museum in the United States is the National Museum of the United States Air Force at Wright-Patterson Air Force Base near Dayton, Ohio. It also has the best military aviation history Web site, www.wpafb.af.mil/museum/index.htm.

For many original documents of the World War II air war, including the 1945 Strategic Bombing Survey, go to www.ibiblio.org/hyperwar/.

For the history of radio news and to actually hear the first bulletins about Pearl Harbor, try "The Old Time Radio" Web site run by James F. Widner at www.otr.com.

The papers of John Leahr and Herb Heilbrun will one day be deposited in a research library and thus made accessible to future historians who might be current readers of this book. In the meantime, the author will take questions at jfleischman@ascb.org, warning everyone that this book already contains nearly everything the author knows about these two black and white airmen.

INDEX